Liturgical Retreat

LITURGICAL RETREAT

Roy J. Howard, S.J.

SHEED AND WARD - NEW YORK

Library of Congress Catalog Card Number 59-10657

IMPRIMI POTEST:

LAWRENCE M. O'NEILL, S.J.

PRAEP. PROV. NEO-ORLEANSIS

NIHIL OBSTAT:

THOMAS J. MCHUGH, LL.D.

CENSOR LIBRORUM

IMPRIMATUR:

✠ JEROME D. HANNAN

BISHOP OF SCRANTON

JUNE 6, 1959

MANUFACTURED IN THE UNITED STATES OF AMERICA

Acknowledgment

The author wishes to express to Mrs. John Moore his thanks for correcting the proofs.

Preface

This book is prompted by the desire to fuse the two most prominent forces acting in our time for the spiritual benefit of the Catholic—the Spiritual Exercises and the Liturgical Movement.

It does not pretend to be a kind of do-it-yourself retreat—though it uses the word in its title—yet it wants to do something of what a retreat wants to do, establish a person more firmly and consciously in his Christ-like way of life. It seeks to do this through reflection upon the meaning of the sacraments of Baptism, Confirmation, and Eucharist.

When St. Ignatius Loyola first offered to others the Spiritual Exercises as what might be described as a sort of ordered context of prayer, he made them the occasion in which a generous person, counting on the help of the Holy Ghost, could decide what he should do with his life. The central moment of the Exercises was and is the "Election." But over the centuries a slight change in accent has taken place in the presentation of this moment, brought on by a change in the condition of people making a retreat (as the practice of the Spiritual Exercises came to be called). In the earliest usages of the retreat, the decision taken at the time of the Election bore normally upon the choice of a state in life: marriage, priesthood, monastery, teacher's rostrum, business career, and so forth. In our own times, a retreat is most often aimed at helping a person put into practice the requirements of the state in life which he has already chosen. The retreatant is asked to see very clearly just who he is and to renew himself in terms of who he is. It is a time of rededication rather than of giving a wholly new orientation to one's life.

But who is the person who makes a retreat?

He is obviously much more than a name picked at random from the pages of the telephone directory. He is more, even, than one whose good will is something above the common measure. He is someone special in God's sight. Why? because he is one of the baptized. This is the root grace which marks him off. It has made him religiously what he is, a child of God and heir of all the good things in the kingdom.

The ten chapters of this book are concerned with the rededication of the Catholic as one of the baptized.

For, if the baptized is someone special in God's sight, then he has certain qualities which are peculiarly his own—qualities of status, function, spiritual life. He did not stumble by accident upon them. He did not pick and choose what they would be nor whether they should be his at all. He received them. They were given over to him in those sacraments which make up what the Fathers of the Church liked to call the baptismal cycle: Baptism, Confirmation, and Holy Eucharist.

These three sacraments are closely connected one with another. In the early Church they were given within a few minutes of each other, sometimes even to babies in their mothers' arms. It was easily understood then that each one calls out for the others and even gives something of what the others give.

There are no doubt many ways in which a person can make a retreat and many purposes which he might have in view, but surely one of the best ways is to relive now, if it is possible, those sacramental events which made him a child of God and heir of the kingdom of heaven. And one of the best purposes must certainly be the realization of the importance these three sacraments have in his life. All the sacraments, and these three in particular, are more than mere sources of grace, they are patterns for using it. What they give is not simply strength but a way of applying it, not simply force but a way of life. They not only enable us to live, they teach us how to do so.

For this reason the sacraments should not be thought of first of all as means to help us live up to the demands of the ten commandments. They do that, of course. But it is not their principal contribution. They do not exist for the sake of the commandments. They exist in their own right. *They,* and not the commandments, are our primary guide to living.

At this point, then, the Ignatian retreat, which seeks a prayerful rededication in a way of life, and the sacraments, especially those of the baptismal cycle, join hands.

We want in retreat to experience in an adult, conscious, and quite deliberate fashion that dedication which was made for us, more likely than not, as children in the decisions of others. Our parents or guardians spoke then, now we will speak for ourselves. We want to ratify on our own account what we once received, probably without our knowing it.

At the center of this dedication lies the Mass. It is there that all the other sacraments have their source and final meeting place.

The guiding principle of these chapters is liturgical piety. The reader will discern, especially if he has himself made retreats, the Ignatian prism through which the different spiritual realities of the sacraments are viewed. Ignatius, as Fr. Hugo Rahner has beautifully shown in his book *The Spirituality of St. Ignatius,* is more than anything else a "man of the Church." It is not simply a question of citing his "Rules for Thinking with the Church" nor even of pointing out his revolutionary insistence upon a return to the frequent Communion of the early Church. On the other hand, neither

is it a question of lending Ignatius the liturgical consciousness of our own day.

It is rather this: Ignatius was a man who had a *sense*
of the Church, a sense of the visible kingdom of God
as a sort of field of force acting within the world and in
which each Catholic himself acts as one both receiving
and giving back the charge of the atmosphere in which
he lives and works. Ignatius burned with the realization
that the Church is a *visible* kingdom, and that consequently one's dedication within it is a visible dedication,
conferred by visible rite, charging with a visible mission,
put into effect by visible means.

Retreat is a time to relive that dedication, step by step.
It would be best, no doubt, to do this in a place given
over entirely to the work of making retreats, where
in silence "one learns that it is at every moment his life
he is passing through." Still, it can be done in the elected
solitude of lying at night propped up in bed, after the
children are asleep and the television set is turned off.
This too can be a context of prayer. Even there the individual Catholic can discover that God has fulfilled
in him the promise made through Ezechiel the prophet;
he may understand better, then, what it means to have
been baptized—

And then I will pour cleansing streams over you, to
purge you from every stain you bear, purge you from
the taint of your idolatry. I will give you a new heart,

and breathe a new spirit into you; I will take away from your breasts those hearts that are hard as stone, and give you human hearts instead. . . .

to have been confirmed—

I will make my spirit penetrate you . . .

and to have received the Holy Eucharist—

You shall be my people, and I will be your God.[1]

---

[1] Ezec. 36:25-28. The Scripture translation used throughout this work is chiefly that of Msgr. Ronald Knox, copyright 1944, 1948, 1950, Sheed & Ward, Inc., New York.

Contents

Liturgical Retreat

Baptism

1. *Descent*

There came one time to see Jesus at night a prominent member of the Sanhedrin, inquiring but afraid. His name was Nicodemus and he spoke in the first person plural: *Master, we know that thou hast come from God to teach us.* It was not a question, but Jesus read the intention behind it: *Believe me when I tell thee this; a man cannot see the kingdom of God without being born anew. . . . No man can enter into the kingdom of God unless birth comes to him from water, and from the Holy Spirit* (John 3:2-3,5).

Nicodemus was our spokesman in those evening conversations. The answers Jesus gave were directed to us. They surprise us even now, almost as much as they did Nicodemus when they were first uttered.

The life Jesus promises is a strange thing. It comes through water and the Holy Spirit. It is a rebirth. It can only be gained by closing off the life we have and beginning again. Somehow, this new living is prefaced by death.

The thought discourages us a little. How much is being asked? We feel so comfortable and so much at home in this skin we know so well. And what lies on the other side of dying? Yet Christ's voice is insistent. . . . *a grain of wheat must fall into the ground and die, or else it remains nothing more than a grain of wheat; but if it dies, then it yields rich fruit* (John 12:24). We are troubled on hearing such words. We find ourselves suddenly able to sympathize with those too hasty enquirers who have turned from the pages of the New Testament thinking Christianity a rather sad affair and Christ an almost morbid prophet.

The facts are clear enough. Christ often speaks of death, of losing one's life, even of hating it, and of being born again. Why this apparently negative insistence? What does it all mean?

We have very little in our environment to prepare us for such notions. Our age teaches us that death, like a socially unacceptable illness, is a tragic and somehow shameful thing. We are urged to cover it up, to talk about it in guarded terms, to let others take care of it and bury it finally out of sight under quilted cushions and a thick layer of cosmetics. Our environment leaves us only one meaning for death—that crushing final separation which will remove us all, one by one, from the familiar conditions of time.

This is death as the pagans have pictured it. It is a shallow notion and, eventually, a false one. It is certainly not the notion of death which Jesus is at pains to underscore in his own life and words.

Christ reminds us that death is one of those oyster-like realities which hide a pearl under a shabby and ugly shell. A richer meaning is concealed for those who take the trouble to look. It is an imperative meaning, not the sort which it would be better for us to know but which we can do rather well without; this meaning lies indispensably at the threshold of our life in grace. *A man cannot see the kingdom of God without being born anew.* Cannot!

In this passage our Lord indicates to us the properly religious dimension of death. He leads us gently to the unsuspected realization that death, from whatever angle it is viewed, is the prelude of every momentous undertaking.

How has this transformation come about, in which death enters into the image of life? To answer this question we must try to discover what really are the lessons death gives us about life.

Death is the moment of summing up. Whatever we have done with ourselves up to that time is caught up in its vortex. Our life has been like a stream. It sprang up somewhere on a valley floor and spread out fingers in search of depressions, ruts, and low places to channel its flow to the sea. It gathered mud, branches, plants, pebbles, and sometimes boulders. It grew. It wound its way down, always down towards the sea. A good geologist might take a cupful of this river water at the point of its spilling into the ocean and tell us, after analysis, where it began and how far it traveled and whether it were a young stream or an old.

Death bends over our lives like the geologist over his stream. All that we bring to this new life is held up for examination. All our story is in those elements, which become now the conditions and factors of change. It is everything we are that enters the crucible of death. Nothing is left out. It can't be. Our new life is for every bit of us. It is meant to affect the whole man.

Because it is total and explicit, death is a lightsome thing. A searchlight across a darkening sky should be its symbol, not a crepe put upon the door, which is a holdover from pre-Christian times, anyway. It is a somewhat cold and harsh light, perhaps, but it is scrupulously fair. It leaves no corners in shadow. It illuminates completely and decisively. It is the light that comes out of eternity. It shows, not what a man ought to be or what he might have been, but what a man is.

The saints knew this. St. Francis wanted to die completely naked, lying on the bare earth. That was not in his eyes a moment for the possible distraction of appearances, much less for shame. His brothers around him granted his request. Nakedness became for him a sacramental, a sign of something sacred. Modesty yielded to a vivid sense of the encompassing presence of God. St. Francis might have prayed in the words of the Hindu poet, Tagore:

> Take, O take—has now become my cry.
> Shatter all from this beggar's bowl; put out
> this lamp of the importunate watcher: hold
> my hands, raise me up from the still gathering
> heap of your gifts into the bare infinity
> of your uncrowded presence.[1]

St. Francis reminds us of those early Christian martyrs whom Tertullian called a people knowing easily how to die. And their example gives us what is perhaps the strangest and the most profound lesson of death, that somehow it is free.

Of course, there is coercion in death. It is punishment for sin, after all, and by definition punishment is something we don't like and would avoid if we could.

But we can choose even that which we cannot avoid. We can choose at least the acceptance of it, submission to it.

There is a story told of a German scholar on his death-bed who received a visit from a doctor, an old friend. The doctor was trying discreetly to help. "Modern science," he said, "can make dying extraordinarily easy for us with pain-killing injections." The dying man

[1] Rabindranath Tagore, *Fruit-Gathering* (New York and London: Macmillan, 1920).

raised himself with painful effort. "Nobody," he said vigorously, "shall deprive me of *my* death." Perhaps it was stubbornness. But then, perhaps it was martyrdom. The point is, it might have been martyrdom.

The last days of Christ's life on earth show us at the approach of death this strange ambivalence between coercion and freedom.

We recall the scene in St. Luke's gospel when Jesus turned his face sorrowfully towards Jerusalem, on that last journey up to the holy city. He knew what lay ahead, as he walked toward it. He had predicted it often enough to his apostles. They had thought it a monstrous idea and even tried to dissuade him from allowing it to happen. But Jesus rebuked them. He did not turn aside his steps.

Later in the garden, with the supreme crisis upon him, he prayed that the cup might pass from him. He confessed his fear, for this was not his hour. He had yielded his mastery of it to the priests of the temple and those shadows behind them who were the emissaries of darkness. But, when they came to the garden entrance, he went out to meet them, and said, *I am he, whom you seek.*

Jesus, who could have had legions of angels in his defense, refused their aid and thereby gave us who cannot have them a decisive lesson. It was not merely the example of his courage; many men have given that example before and after him. It was the lesson that death is the condition of life, and that he who would rise with Christ must first of all freely descend with him into the tomb.

We must probe a bit deeper, for Christ's using the imagery of death is not principally concerned with that last and most dramatic moment of leave-taking of this world; the death Christ speaks of takes place during life, every day. It is a dying Christ referred to when he said that, to follow him, one must take up his cross daily.

After all, death is not such a stranger to life. There is a little of it present all along, not merely a lot of it at life's close. It is not poetic exaggeration to say that we meet a foreshadowing of it in deciding, for example, to crawl on a winter's morning out of a warm bed; we have slain our sleep. And the priest—has he not died to wife, children, home? The family man—has he not died to a carefree life of adventure, his decisions shaped only by his own whims and the turns of fate? It is along the pathways of freedom that death takes up a position in the process of life, for every choice is a death of sorts. Every choice *is*—not entails merely—a renunciation, for it is the pruning of desire and possibility and even expectancy in favor of a single, perhaps small, yet real achievement. Every choice is an abandoning, a separation, a leave-taking. It is a little demise. It was a wise Frenchman who wrote, "To say good-bye is to die a little bit."

It is obvious that this type of death does not wait

until the end of our lives before making itself felt. It is everywhere present, both as something forced upon us and as something desired. In each case it is a highly personal thing. It engages that core of ourselves where we mold an individual eternity. There is something stubborn about it, a certain impassive relentlessness. We *may* choose? Yes, we know that. But more than that, we *must* choose. Such death cannot be avoided. There is no other way of shaping our personalities. We do not have the opportunity to repeat simply the patterns of the past, living out our lives by instinct, the way a cat can. Choice is the inescapable crucible of our inner self; instinct is of no help here. And choice always comes in terms of crisis.

> The undecided and the dilettante never know the robust testing of choice, by which the psychic muscles acquire their tone. Here the narrow experience of aggressiveness is transformed into the essential experience of confrontation, the vital face to face, which always comes back by some detour, to a face to face with death.[2]

Dr. Mounier is speaking here as a psychiatrist, but as a psychiatrist who has read quite correctly the human heart. He helps us to understand that the world is already judged and that Christ is continually coming into it to stand before each one of us announcing that who-

[2] Emmanuel Mounier, *The Character of Man*, trans. Cynthia Rowland (New York: Harper & Brothers, 1956), p. 211.

ever is not with him is against him. And saying, *Choose!*

This is the truest, the religious meaning of death, and it sometimes carries with it its own special sadness. But at any rate it is not something outside life and extrinsic to it. Death is a part of life, an old friend in the process of change and growth, a partaker of life and, in the long run, one of its noblest ingredients. "Life is changed, not taken away," reads the preface of the Requiem Mass. If that last leave-taking is the most dramatic and revolutionary of all, it is only because it is growth at its most decisive stage.

But, philosophical musings on the meaning of death are not, after all, the main reason for its becoming the image and prelude of a new life. It is not philosophy which St. Paul had in mind when he wrote that we were buried together with Christ. The Christian man in St. Paul's view is one who prolongs in his own life and within the stream of his own choices the mystery of Christ's redemptive life, death, and resurrection. This is the fundamental reason that our life in grace should begin by a death to our former selves—the "old man," as St. Paul called him. It is because Christ died. So then must we. It is as simple as that. There is no other way. In order to live really, or rather in order to have Christ living in us, we must be in our degree baptized with that baptism with which Christ was baptized. We must even try to make ourselves "impatient for its accomplishment."

This was not something new which Christ introduced
into God's plan. It had always been so.

When God first began his mysterious and special
presence in history he chose for himself a people despised
by the other nations. He bade them leave the land of
Egypt, a land of monumental culture and progress,
where the Hebrews might in time have bettered their
condition. He sent them into the desert, into the vast
emptiness and solitude of those unknown and hence
fearful wastes. This was a death, and the people did not
like it very much. They grumbled. They longed for the
fleshpots of Egypt. They complained often and loudly.

Forty years God kept them in the desert. The trek
from Egypt to Chanaan need hardly have taken so
much time. Why did God keep them there so long? It
was not till two generations later, when those originally
beginning the journey had died, that God sent Joshua
and his men against Jericho and then beyond into the
plains of the Promised Land. Joshua and Caleb were the
only two of the original band to set foot upon the heritage God had promised. God intended it that way.[3] Not
an individual merely, a whole people had to die in order
that Israel might be born.

When Jesus began his public ministry his first act
was in conscious imitation of that initial intervention
of God into history. Jesus was led into the desert by the
Spirit, St. Luke tells us. There he was to retrace in his

[3] Num. 14:27-35.

own person the trials which were once the prelude to
the possession of the Promised Land and now would be
the prelude to establishing the kingdom. Was it coercion
that the Holy Spirit exercised upon Jesus? No, it was
a leading on, fully ratified by Christ's own choice.

The apostles in their turn began their missionary life
in imitation of their master. After Jesus' Ascension they
retired into the upper room, not out of fear, but to await
prayerfully the coming of the Holy Spirit.

We have good reason to believe that St. Paul, too,
prefaced his apostolate with a period of solitude in the
Arabian desert.

In every case we find that renunciation, separation,
withdrawal are the preludes to great undertakings.

God's special servants in our own day carry on that
tradition. We may catch ourselves wondering sometimes
about those young men and women who trip lightly off
to some granite cloister and thereafter are allowed to
have contact even with their family only through
the frankly discouraging filter of a grill. We learn that
some contemplatives have never seen automobiles, those
at least who have been in the cloister long enough and
who have not had to venture outside the cloister walls
for health or other reasons. (But they see airplanes, flying
above their gardens. The sky is open to them.) Is it so
strange, after all? Have not these religious simply done
now of their own free will what each of us will one day
be forced to do, like it or not?

The theme of death is, then, a religious constant in God's dealings with his people. Withdrawal, separation, leave-taking, renunciation—these are the necessary preludes to every great religious undertaking. Not for their own sakes, however, but as the initial step in an immensely satisfying journey.

Holy Mother Church has not lost sight of the lesson. Lent is her annual retreat, her retiring from distraction to prepare for Easter.

When we make a retreat we repeat on our own account this gesture of the liturgical year. We draw back awhile, we retire, we die a little bit. We enter into a period of solitude, seeking a silence not merely of the body and of external activity but of the soul as well. We prune away the distractions that clutter and conceal our daily living. We take time-out, in order to observe, to be attentive, to see ourselves, the world around us, and, most especially, God. In solitude we learn who we are.

Above all, remember this that I tell you: pay attention. Give your full attention to everything you do, everything you hear. You will discover new worlds. . . . There is no thing or person that cannot teach you something. . . . We move like automatons. That is a mistake. There must be reflection. . . .

If you pay attention—and don't think that all these theories are mine: they are St. Augustine's—you will dis-

cover something very important: harmony. You will
realize that there is a harmony in everything, that everything forms part of a harmonious whole. . . . Talking,
one was deceived by the world; keeping silent, one paid
attention. . . .[4]

But like Christ going into the desert and like the
apostles and Paul in their withdrawal, we enter upon
the leave-taking of our retreat by our own free choice.
We choose to lay ourselves down naked, like St. Francis.
But—and this is the significant point—we have been
here before. Even if this is our first regular retreat, we
have experienced this before. Another day, in our childhood, our godparents loosened the baby garments around
our neck; we were anointed, the waters closed over us,
and we died.

You know well enough that we who were taken up into
Christ by baptism have been taken up, all of us, into his
death. In our baptism, we have been buried with him,
died like him, that so, just as Christ was raised up by his
Father's power from the dead, we too might live and
move in a new kind of existence. (Rom. 6:3-4)

Retreat is a deliberate re-enactment of that death
which took place for us in sacramental sign when we had
no personal exercise of our wills.

[4] In Gironella's novel, *The Cypresses Believe in God* (trans. Harriet
de Onis; New York: Knopf, 1955), a confessor gives this advice to
a young penitent trying to break off an affair.

Retreat takes us back to Baptism, to the sacrament which St. Cyril of Jerusalem called a sepulchre and a mother. He called it that in a catechetical instruction given to his converts in the Church of the Holy Sepulchre itself, with the sacred mementos of Christ's burial all around him. St. Cyril said,

> . . . you were led to the holy pool of divine baptism, as Christ was led to the sepulchre which lies before you. And each of you was asked whether he believed in the name of the Father, and of the Son, and of the Holy Spirit. And you made that saving confession, and descended a third time into the water, and ascended again; here, too, portraying by way of likeness the three days' burial of Christ. . . . At one and the same moment you were dying and being born, and that saving water became at once your grave and your mother.[5]

They were not Cyril's original ideas. Not all the logic of the Greeks nor the mysteries of the Persians could have led him to say them. These ideas had another source:

Believe me when I tell thee this; a man cannot see the kingdom of God without being born anew. (John 3:3)

He alone triumphs over the world, who believes that Jesus is the Son of God. He it is, Jesus Christ, whose coming has been made known to us by water and blood;

[5] *Sources of Christian Theology;* vol. i, *Sacraments and Worship,* ed. Paul F. Palmer, S.J. (Westminster: The Newman Press, 1955), p. 13.

water and blood as well, not water only. . . . (I John
5:5-6)

Water and blood. There is in scriptural and liturgical
statements about Baptism an enduring preoccupation
with death. But it is not morbidity which put it there,
for this death is the prelude to momentous happenings.
On the other hand, it is not an abstract or general type
of death which is spoken of. This is an historical death,
the death of a person, the death of Christ.

One who comes to the baptismal font is faced first of
all with this death to the world which Christ experienced; he must somehow make it his own:

"Do you renounce Satan?" the priest asks on the
threshold of the church.

"I do renounce him," answers the neophyte, or his
godparents for him.

"And all his works?"

"I do renounce them."

"And all his display?"

"I do renounce it."

It is after this solemn separation from what we
have been, this abandonment of an old familiar way of
living, that we turn our faces to the kingdom and are
led into the church itself, to be baptized.

2. *Beginnings*

God, at the beginning of time, created heaven and earth. Earth was still an empty waste, and darkness hung over the deep; but already, over its waters, stirred the breath of God. (Gen. 1:1-2)

We cannot help thinking, when we approach the baptismal font, of that fluid but formless mass over which in the beginning of time hovered the Spirit of God. It was the way the author of Genesis pictured to himself the nothingness out of which God created. It was a stuff without shape or meaning, an empty and restless sea. Under God's action it became the matrix of life. The waters of our baptism remind us of it.

In order to understand our new birth in Christ, we must also understand what that first birth in the beginning of the world was meant to be. Our reflection uncovers two lessons—the dignity of man, and the charge which even in the beginning was laid upon him.

It happened then that in the simple majesty of his

word God created all of heaven and earth. When God spoke, the seas parted to reveal the land, the harsh brown earth softened with the green of grasses and trees. At his voice, the seas swam with life, the forests echoed to animal cries, the skies were crisscrossed by many birds in flight. And God saw that all this was good, in fact that it was very good.

But God had a particular interest in the waters. He arranged for one of those streams recently channeled to spring up in a place called Eden, a land said vaguely to be somewhere to the East. It was such a mighty stream that it flowed off from its source in four rivers, which in their turn irrigated with their plentiful waters the whole extent of the garden of Eden. In fact, these rivers made it a garden, for it is clear that the writer of Genesis thought of this region as a marvelous oasis, a verdant refuge set in the midst of burning desert wastes. Four rivers to water it! No wonder the garden seemed beautiful.

Into this privileged spot God would put Adam and Eve.

How did God create our first parents?

That God is the origin of absolutely everything is in itself a difficult enough notion to express, but for the writer of Genesis the task of expressing it was made doubly hard because he wanted to show that God was specially involved in the creation of man, more so, though the thought strikes us as strange at first, than in the creation of other things in the universe. To other creatures God is master, to man he is Father. That is why the writer of Genesis presents God to us, not as standing off at a distance and forming man merely by a lordly word of command—as God had formed the other creatures—but as coming down into his creation, becoming strangely involved in it, giving it a share in his immense activity. The all-spiritual God is pictured as stooping down by a river bank in the garden of Eden and digging out with his fingers a mass of clay. He packs it and kneads it. He shapes it into the body of a man. He smoothes it and arranges it on the ground. That is what the verb means, "God *formed* man." It was a potter's work upon clay. Even at a later date when Hebrew theology was more precise, this expressive metaphor was respectfully kept, because it contained for those who read it correctly a ground of trust:

> It was thy hand that made me, no part of me but is thy fashioning; and wilt thou cast me aside all in a moment? Thou the craftsman, though of clay thy handiwork, and must all be ground to dust again? (Job 10:8-9)

It is true that God is only forming man's body, but the scene in Genesis shows us that God does it with careful attention and even with affection, as would an artisan who puts all his talent and skill into his work. Because he loves his work. God is proud of the work of his hands.

But man's soul has not yet been given to him.

How did God give man a soul?

He did not draw back and command, as Michelangelo stepped back from his "Moses" and cried "Speak!"

He did not look around in his creation to find some already existing matter out of which a soul might be fashioned, as he had found the clay from which to fashion man's body.

Rather, God bent over this lifeless shape at his feet, and from the depths of his own spiritual and immortal being God breathed into the clay a soul.

So it is that, though all other creatures in the universe are lovely, only man is the image and likeness of God. All other creatures are relative to man. Man alone is an end in himself. All other creatures are things. Man is a person.

Hence, with the coming of man into the world, all the rest of creation takes on mind and meaning. Before this the universe was merely matter. It could not find within itself any point of contact with the spirit world of God, until man supplied the bridge. The administration of man was needed for creation to offer true praise to God.

This leads to a consideration of the commission which man therefore has, as lord and administrator of creation.

Man can perform his task in the world, raising creatures to the point of praise, only because he is himself rooted in matter. His very name means taken from the ground. Man is himself a part of the world of matter,

not by any means a stranger to it. He cannot flee it in
some sort of weird angelism. He must always be on his
guard to resist the Platonic temptation which would
lead him to think that he can set up house in some other,
less refractory world. Man is himself matter. That is
his nature. He must come to grips with matter, not
merely in order to fulfill creation, but in order to fulfill
himself. There is no other way.

But man comes to grips with matter in a spirit of joy
and gratitude and even of reverence. Job tells us that the
sons of god—that is, the angels—raised on the morning
of creation *a joyful melody* (Job 38:7). Man, who was
created a little less than the angels, can do the same.
Man is one who can translate, so to speak, the aspirations
of the universe into the language of God.

We, of course, have inherited Adam's charge. There
must be, in order for us to fulfill it, something of St.
Francis in our make-up. The saint of Assisi had the grace
of finding a personal dimension in every cranny of
creation. It was *Sister Death* and *Brother Wolf* and *his
friends* the birds. It was poverty that opened up for him
this inner world. St. Francis did not keep his joy to
himself. He sent his brothers as missionaries into the Um-
brian hills and gave them orders to preach in the village
squares. What was their text? They sang the "Song of
the Sun," and in return for their labors they asked con-
version.

Most high omnipotent good Lord,

Thine are the praises, the glory, the honor, and all
    benediction.

To thee alone, Most High, do they belong,

And no man is worthy to mention thee.

Praised be thou, my Lord, with all thy creatures,

Especially the honored Brother Sun,

Who makes the day and illumines us through thee.

And he is beautiful and radiant with great splendor

Bears the stamp [*significatione*] of thee, Most High One.

Praised be thou, my Lord, for Sister Moon and the stars,

Thou hast formed them in heaven clear and precious and
    beautiful.

Praised be thou, my Lord, for Brother Wind,

And for the air, and cloudy and clear and every weather,

By which thou givest sustenance to thy creatures.

Praised be thou, my Lord, for Sister Water,

Which is very useful and humble and precious and chaste.

Praised be thou, my Lord, for Brother Fire,

By whom thou lightest the night,

And he is beautiful and jocund and robust and strong.

Praised be thou, my Lord, for our sister Mother Earth,

Who sustains and governs us,

And produces various fruits with colored flowers and
    herbage.

Praise and bless my Lord and give him thanks

And serve him with great humility.[1]

---

[1] The Italian text together with the English translation may be
found in Johannes Jorgensen, *Saint Francis of Assisi* (New York:
Longmans, Green and Co., 1912), pp. 313-314.

God did not in the beginning intend the world to be the enemy of man, a hobble on his efforts, a prison to his ambitions. There is no reason to echo the mournful tones of Camus' hero in *The Fall*: "We shall never escape from this immense baptismal font which is the world." Who wants to escape from it? To face it is man's destiny, as well as his challenge and even his danger. "This life is a glorious fight," wrote Chesterton, "but a miserable truce."

This additional facet of man's relation to the world must be carefully weighed: that man is not put into the world to contemplate but to work it, to dig it, to achieve it. If it is true that creation cannot get to God without man, it is equally certain that man cannot get to God without creation.

The blessing of God upon his newly formed human couple was not a reward. It was a commission. *Increase and multiply and fill the earth, and make it yours* (Gen. 1:28). Even before the fall it was man's destiny to organize the world; from the beginning that was his life's task. *So the Lord God took man and put him in his garden of delight, to cultivate and tend it* (Gen. 2:15).

Man was from the beginning called to be a workman in the world along with God. The charge is on him yet, and especially on us whom God has renewed. *You are a field of God's tilling, a structure of God's design; and we are only his assistants,* wrote St. Paul (I Cor. 3:9), the tent-maker, to the Corinthians, though here he was speaking in particular of his apostolic labors. There is no room for idleness in God's house, whether the Church or the world. Paul put it bluntly for those who in becoming Christians had pooled their material resources: *the man who refuses to work must be left to starve* (II Thess. 3:10). The reason for Paul's intransigence is not some sort of popular contract fit to edify the sociologists of these past few decades. The reason is simply that God himself has worked in the world from the beginning, creating it, conserving it, renewing it. *Lord, you fill your city with joy in the enormous flowing of your grace; you push forth the baptismal spring, to renew all the nations of the earth,* says the ritual of Baptism. And man is made in the image and likeness of God. He is God's image not merely as spirit but as creator.

There isn't any corner of God's green earth which can escape this commission entrusted to man. Run through the list of blessings given in the priest's ritual: for rosaries, sick animals, stables, cornerstones, holy pictures, automobiles, tanks (military), pregnant women, etc. You will find there a blessing for everything (except, as one astute wag remarked, an idea). And how human it all is!

It takes time, of course. Angels can dispose of their destinies in one all-embracing decision. But then, they are pure spirits and have in them no principle of quantity or time or progression. But man is matter. He works his way in little dibs and dabs, slowly, adding gradually to the canvas of his life, color by color.

But here is the point of danger. Matter is of its nature

divisive, extenuating, opaque. There is an ambiguity in it, for it speaks of God but hides him at the same time. Because it speaks of him it solicits our reverence, because it hides him it can become our idol. Man must be wary in approaching matter. It can only be a stepping-stone for him, not an end in itself.

The reason is this. To say that man's soul comes directly from God, without the intermediary of anything in this world, is to say the first part of a sentence whose second part goes like this: . . . and therefore man, by that which makes him what he is and gives him special rank among creatures, can find the equal of himself nowhere in creation. No item in creation, not even his fellow man, can fill up the hunger of his soul. "Man has a homesickness for God," wrote Sabatier. It is true. Whatever creature man works with or loves, he aims at God. Man loves God in all his loves.

During the blessing of the batismal water on Holy Saturday night, the Church prays in the psalmist's words:

O God, my whole soul longs for thee, as a deer for running water. My whole soul thirsts for the living God: shall I never make my pilgrimage into his presence . . .?

And St. Augustine often echoed the thought. "O God, I am, until I rest in thee, a burden unto myself."

It is perhaps true that many people do not feel this

deep yearning for God, young people especially. They say they don't. These people serve to remind us that creatures are good, that they came from God and go back to him, that they have something of God in them and can quite easily therefore absorb all man's conscious striving. These people invite us, in addition, to reflect upon the fact that this yearning for God is not a matter of feeling, or even necessarily a conscious thing, but rather a deeper, expanding center of ourselves which we can either heed or ignore, as we will, but not annihilate.

We live too much at the tips of our fingers, on the fringes of our existence, filling our hands, thinking thereby to satisfy our hearts. We work from outside in.

Happiness comes rather from the inside and works out. It is the soul suffusing our earthly occupation with meaning for itself and for us as we go on the road to God. Man is put into the world to organize it, but himself first of all. He must learn to see God as the unifying principle of his multifarious activity, and love God in all his loves. St. Augustine knew this:

> Nor in all these things that my mind traverses in search of you, O God, do I find any rest for my spirit save in you, in whom all that is scattered in me is brought into one.[2]

---

[2] This sentence of St. Augustine is reminiscent of another of Christ and rings in, therefore, a still richer tone: "*He who is not with me is against me; he who does not gather his store with me scatters it abroad* (Matt. 12:30).

And again: "O Beauty, ever ancient, ever new, too late
have I loved *thee*." That is the point. We tumble down
to God at the center of our world like a stone to the
center of gravity. To have loved many things before
having loved God is always a pity, and sometimes a
tragic pity.

From the primordial waters God drew a world which
needed to be cared for and cultivated and even protected.
Into this world God put man, that strange ambivalent
creature whose feet tread so heavily upon the ground
but whose head is in the clouds. We do not know
whether to define him as rational animal or incarnate
spirit. We ask ourselves, as he enters the baptismal
waters, to which world does he belong really? He stands
midway between what is purely matter and what is
purely spirit. He is the mediator and priest of creation.
He has limbs and senses in common with other creatures
of the world, but he alone can use them in gestures of
reverence and of prayer.

The primordial waters are not merely those of the beginning of time. They are all those waters which mark
a new beginning, and over which hovers the Spirit of
God. Out of them comes a whole world that has to be
achieved.

3. Satan

In blessing the baptismal water on Holy Saturday night the celebrant divides the water with his hand in the sign of the Cross and says:

> May this water, prepared for the rebirth of men, be rendered fruitful by the secret inpouring of his divine power. . . . Begone then every unclean spirit at thy bidding, Lord; begone all wickedness and satanic wiles. Let no power of opposition intrude here, or spread its snares about this place, or creep into it by stealth, or taint it by its poison.

He then touches the water with his hand and says:

> May this holy and innocent creature be free from all the enemy's assaults and cleansed by the removal of all wickedness.

In the sacramental life of the Church it often happens that blessings include in their formula an exorcism. The

bits of creation which are to be the vehicles of God's
grace must first of all be freed from an unholy presence.
It is the same with the blessing of salt used at Baptism,
with the oil for the use of the sick. The ritual gives us
many other examples: the blessing of bread, of fountains,
of wells, of ovens, etc. Even the cross which each of us
traces on his forehead with holy water when entering
the church is an echo of the exorcist's cry: "Behold the
cross of the Lord! Depart, every inimical faction!"

In this chapter we take our cue from those exorcisms.
We need to remind ourselves that something has gone
wrong with our world.

How did it happen? The world as it came fresh and
new from the hands of God had been an object even of
the divine satisfaction; he saw that it was good, that it
was very good. But now . . .?

. . . *and the farmer's men went to him and said, Sir,
was it not clean seed thou didst sow in thy field? How
comes it, then, that there are tares in it? He said, An
enemy has done it* (Matt. 13:27-28).

There is a difference between the world which God
created and the one in which we live, a difference which
Satan has brought about. Because of him, something
has gone wrong with our world.

It was not so in the beginning. When we turn to
Genesis for a picture of God's relations with man before
the fall, we find them indicated by the writer in language which is well adapted to bring out the intimate

friendship Adam and Eve enjoyed with God. God is said to have come into the garden at the close of the day as though coming to visit with Adam and Eve, as though coming to stroll along with them in familiar conversation. It shows us plainly the regard God had for these privileged creatures, then still touched with grace.

But Satan came one day into the garden as well, in the guise of a creature, a friend. Here was an angelic intellect come to try his wiles on man and woman. He did not have to rack his brain to find the temptation most suitable for the occasion. He spotted the right one in a flash. A little question of presentation, perhaps. The precise content was clear. It still surprises us to learn what it was.

Would you like to be like God?

It sounds exaggerated, foolishly so. But is it?

Man was created in the image and likeness of God. Grace, which our first parents had in abundance, is a participation in the divine nature. At a later date Christ would tell us that we must imitate the perfection of his Father. There is in man a beginning of a divine similarity. It is a beginning only. And it is a gift, a pure gift. But Satan said, "This is yours. You deserve it. You can put it to work for you. No point in letting it lie around fallow."

To be like God? To control, to master, to have others dependent upon you, to feel yourself the focus of all eyes, to direct others, to manipulate them, to judge?

That was Satan's temptation, that man should bend
creatures away from their reference to God and turn
them in upon himself instead. And, of course, it was a
lie. God's nature is not like that, as Jesus would so plainly
show. To be like God is not to be a self-centered megalo-
maniac. But our first parents did not have the lesson of
Christ's life before them. They fell into Satan's trap,
Eve in a confused and hasty manner, Adam with somewhat more deliberation—and regret.

Our first parents were not long in realizing that, with
that first surrender, something had gone wrong with
their world. Shame is the proof of it. They hid themselves. Because they had disobeyed their Father and
friend? Yes, but also because they saw their nakedness
and realized they had lost the gift of rational control
over appetite. They were not only separated from God,
they were interiorly divided; they were no longer the
masters of themselves. This internal division soon had
its counterpart in their relations with the world. It had
always been man's task to till the soil. God had put him
into the garden for that purpose. But now he would till
it in the sweat of his brow. The world would turn
towards him a resisting and intractable side. This in-
ability to master the world would in turn heighten man's
incapacity to master himself. It was a downward slope
upon which Adam had stepped and time would only
add speed to his fall.

St. Paul sums up the effects of Adam's sin in a single

word: *death. It was through one man that guilt came into the world; and since death came owing to guilt, death was handed on to all mankind by one man* (Rom. 5:12).

St. Paul means much more here than physical death. Physical death is itself merely the symptom of a more awful presence, a sort of pervasive force working for our spiritual death. Just as surely as we are subject to physical death, we are subject to that force. We have inherited from our first parents the same situation which led them to hide from God and clothe themselves in creaturely trappings. The river which welled up in the garden, from which we all drink, was meant to be a river of life. It has become polluted at its source. Now every creature has been infected by its waters.

Something has gone wrong with our world.

Would we think so, if we took the trouble to tot up some of the moral lessons of history? It would be rash to answer this question with too great assuredness, whichever side be taken. But we may not, at any rate, assume naive faith in an inevitable progress, as some did a few years ago. Whatever may be the final interpretation of history, *that* at least is not it. How do we read our times?

A war was fought to end war, and then it was concluded with a treaty which made peace impossible.

It was taken for granted that democracy marked the most enlightened of man's political achievements, and then the world watched in dismay as two democracies voted themselves into dictatorships. Even now, in the assemblies of some traditionally democratic nations, anti-democratic parties hold a strong disruptive power and threaten seriously not merely to thwart—which they have long done—but to liquidate democratic opposition.

We thought at least that science would help us live longer. And of course, it has, if we discount the capacity man now has to pulverize his cities and make of entire nations a wasteland. We are shocked to learn that strategy is now discussed in terms of "overkilling." Let it be said to their honor, even the discoverers of atomic power have recoiled from their achievement. Not because they distrust the atom. They distrust man. "A part of us," wrote an editorial writer in the *New York Times*, "never came down from the tree, never crawled out of the cave." We have not kept pace, morally, with our scientific achievements.

What kind of world is ours, when the concept of liquidation has been applied not merely among thieves by one rumrunner to another, but by governments, some of them elected, to vast percentages of their citizenry? Liquidation is not punishment, conquest, or even execution. It is, as Josef Pieper has written,[1] the destruction

[1] Josef Pieper, *Justice*, trans. L. E. Lynch (New York: Pantheon, 1955), p. 26.

of another simply because he is "an other," and hence a rival.

In our country, hardly a national magazine is published which does not have within its covers an appeal by some organization for a contribution towards the support of an orphaned child in Greece or Korea, a displaced person in Germany, a refugee in France. We have grown used to those appeals, and to the pictures of long files of DP's standing like cattle before the soup kitchen or sitting, their faces drained of hope, on the wooden and wire bunks of internment camps.

A commission of the United Nations has told us that one half the people of this world are undernourished. That means that every day one half the people of this world either do not sit down to a meal at all or rise up from one they have taken still feeling hungry.

We don't have to go far afield. There is an economic and social servitude which we brush against every day in our environment. We can hardly claim that social injustice is a subtle problem. The signs of it are too graphic and too widespread. But how explain, then, the cancerous growth of organizations, one of whose conditions of entry is an oath to disenfranchise, to oppress, to frustrate a minority group of their fellow men and women as they try to improve themselves? Is this progress? It is, on the contrary, degradation. But it goes on swimmingly in our world. The Little Rock affair was only one manifestation of our inhumanity to our fellow man, and this now famous incident only proved one thing, as Harry Ashmore, editor of the *Arkansas Gazette*, wrote in a national magazine: that if soldiers could keep nine Negroes out of a public high school, soldiers could get them in again. In neither case was the problem approached in a manner calculated to make us smile upon our world.

Some time ago the Freudian school of thought offered mankind a new salvation in terms of the Reality Principle and of adjustment. It has only been recently that we have been wondering whether what we are adjusting to is worth adjusting to. The Freudians claimed to have brought our problems out into the open, and in many cases they were quite right. Our problems were brought out into the open, and there they are today, as much as ever, out in the open, big as life, still unsolved. However, even to be forced to see them is an advance, and we could find there a real ray of hope, if only our Freudian friends gave the barest inkling of a willingness to consider Christianity a possible solution to the problem. They don't, however, for, in a judgment which they have inherited but never put to the test, they say that Christianity has failed. Chesterton's answer comes to mind: Christianity was not tried and found wanting, it was found difficult and not tried.

The success of evil and the defeat of good have never been so clearly known or so widely publicized as today. Has the knowledge stiffened our determination? On the contrary. It has been left to our age to erect despair into a philosophy and pretend that men can live by it. "Hell," wrote Sartre, "is—other people!"

By how much can our world escape Paul's bitter denunciation of the Romans?

And as they scorned to keep God in their view, so God has abandoned them to a frame of mind worthy of all scorn, that prompts them to disgraceful acts. They are versed in every kind of injustice, knavery, impurity, avarice, and ill-will; spiteful, murderous, contentious, deceitful, depraved, backbiters, slanderers, God's enemies; insolent, haughty, vainglorious; inventive in wickedness, disobedient to their parents; without prudence, without honour, without love, without loyalty, without pity. Yet, with the just decree of God before their minds, they never grasped the truth that those who so live are deserving of death; not only those who commit such acts, but those who countenance such a manner of living. (Rom. 1:28-32)

This is our world, the only one we have, the one over which God gave us charge. It is the atmosphere we breathe, a sort of smog from which we cannot seem to emerge. Only man can restore creation to its rightful place in God's plan, by using it to praise God, instead of using it to praise man.

There's the rub. Man, too, is a part of the world. He cannot point to something around him and disclaim all affinity with it. This pervasive death of which St. Paul speaks has got inside man. It settles there in his heart like lead, weighing him down. The death inside us Paul calls concupiscence. It invades every portion of man's being.

It brings a darkness into our intellect. Prejudices obscure a sound ability to judge. We insist that our opinion of the moment is incontrovertibly the best one. We really believe that it is so. We can hardly bring ourselves to reflect that those who oppose us may not be few, nor stupid, nor malevolent.

Even when we pride ourselves on our loyalty to our faith, how difficult, nevertheless, we find it to accept an opinion—especially a moral opinion—of the Church or her representatives when it goes against the accepted or the desired practice. This, of course, is no plea for a slavish Catholicism; our faith must seek its own understanding; reflection is the homage given by our minds to our faith, the only homage the mind can give. But when the faith speaks in unpleasant terms, how many reasons suddenly pop to the surface of our thinking! It is a constant in human living that we believe what we want to believe, like the somewhat deaf persons who hear nevertheless what they want to hear.

But, what is worse, even when we have correctly judged the course of action which we should adopt, we can't seem to bring ourselves to set out upon it. We know something we do is wrong, some habit that we have is shameful and debilitating and lacking in trust, but we can't seem to bring ourselves to relinquish it. *Praiseworthy intentions are always ready to hand, but I cannot find my way to the performance of them; it is not the good my will prefers, but the evil my will disapproves, that I find myself doing* (Rom. 7:18-19). If we were as honest as St. Paul, we would second this confession. Something has gone wrong inside us. There is a pull there, a steady veering from the path that leads to holiness and to truth.

Would it be too strong to say that the image of our world is the crowd standing in the street looking up to a window ledge of a building high above it where some poor deranged specimen of humanity cringes?—and from the crowd a voice rises, "Go ahead and jump," Did we say that? Did we think it?

Something has gone wrong with our world. Something has gone wrong inside us. Sin has entered the world. Death and concupiscence are the heralds of its presence, the sure warnings of its power. The thought of it was so real to St. Paul that he spoke of Adam's sin as though it had become itself a personal thing, an awful presence stalking our every free action, breathing around us an atmosphere of death.

But we must not imagine Satan behind every misfortune and evil deed in the world. He has gone underground. That is his nice achievement. Why should he show his face? The candidate does not bother appearing

in the state where the vote is assured. The generals do
not get into the front lines as long as the battle is going
well. Satan is taking a personal rest, the organization
gets along fine without him.

It must be admitted, however, that all the evidence of
ignorance, malice, selfishness, depravity, sensuality, suffering, wars, famine, earthquake, and frustration—
that all this in the long run doesn't really do justice to
what St. Paul means when he writes to the Romans that
sin has entered the world. Only our faith can tell us that.

Who can read the pages of the gospels and fail to see
the malignant force which was working against Jesus?

Why dost thou meddle with us, Jesus, son of God?
the two fierce creatures asked our Lord as he stepped
off Peter's boat to begin his preaching among the Gera-
senes (Matt. 8:28-29).

Jesus surrendered himself to the priests and the temple
guards with the words, *But your time has come now, and
darkness has its will* (Luke 22:53).

Nowhere, however, so clearly as at the Last Supper
did our Lord tell us that something has gone wrong with
our world:

> If the world hates you, be sure that it hated me before
> it learned to hate you. If you belonged to the world, the
> world would know you for its own and love you; it is
> because you do not belong to the world, because I have
> singled you out from the midst of the world, that the

world hates you. . . . They will persecute you just as they
have persecuted me; they will pay the same attention to
your words as to mine. (John 15:18-20)

It is for these I pray; I am not praying for the world,
but for those whom thou hast entrusted to me; they belong to thee; as all I have is thine, and all thou hast is
mine. . . . I am remaining in the world no longer, but
they remain in the world, while I am on my way to
thee. Holy Father, keep them true to thy name. . . . I
have given them thy message, and the world has nothing
but hatred for them, because they do not belong to the
world, as I, too, do not belong to the world. I am not
asking that thou shouldst take them out of the world,
but that thou shouldst keep them clear of what is evil.
They do not belong to the world, as I, too, do not belong
to the world. . . . (John 17:9-11, 14-17)

But do we believe it, after all? Christ said, *A man
cannot be the slave of two masters at once; either he will
hate the one and love the other, or he will devote himself
to one and despise the other. You must serve God or
money; you cannot serve both* (Matt. 6:24).

Can't we? Haven't we set it rather as the goal of our
lives to make the best out of both worlds? And if that
is true, do we really believe there is something wrong
with our world?

The early Christians, our forebears in the faith, knew
better. They knew what it meant to renounce Satan.
Those pomps and displays—they saw those every day—

the circuses, the pagan festivals, the ordinary fare of Roman life. And they knew the seriousness of that pledge. They sometimes offered the Eucharistic sacrifice in the catacombs, over the tombs of those who had died for that pledge, who had died rather than compromise.

The world could not change them. It could not even understand them. Most of all it could not bear their presence.

4. Sorrow

Our world has tried to get along without God, without having him as background and foundation. The organization and use of creatures have been carried on in deliberate denial of their reference to God. This is not merely an injustice, it is a sacrilege.

It reminds us of Baltassar. He was the Babylonian king whom the Book of Daniel describes as he entertained one evening in his palace (Dan. 5). More than a thousand friends, courtiers, and hangers-on were present. The celebration grew more and more lively. The king, boastful in his cups, called for the sacred vessels which had been stolen from the temple in Jerusalem after the capture of the Holy City. These objects, consecrated to the temple service, were put upon the banquet tables and were used for the drunken revels of Baltassar and his court. And then, suddenly, upon the wall of the festive chamber, a moving finger wrote judgment in letters of fire.

Perhaps in the long-range providence of God, the threat of atomic destruction will be for us the warning which Baltassar received that night. It may lead us to reflect upon ourselves.

"Depart from him, unclean spirit, and give place to the Holy Spirit, the Paraclete," prays the baptismal ritual. It is not merely, nor chiefly, the water, oil, and salt which must be exorcised; it is ourselves. The long, sordid history of sin, which reflection upon our world reveals to us, is not some extraneous story; it is the echo on a global scale of what we ourselves have done. It is our story.

Doctors are sometimes fond of saying that there is no such thing as sickness, only sick people. So, too, there is no such thing as sin, only sinners. And we are the sinners. The atmosphere of death was born in us, but after that we have, on our own, made it welcome. To pray for realization of this is the purpose of this chapter. It is not a morbid purpose. We want to see how it is that we have met Christ often in our lives, but then turned, perhaps sadly, away from him.

In the second Book of Kings we find the classic statement of man's realization that he is a sinner. It happened in the days when a king's word was law. David was king, one whom God had especially chosen. He was at the height of his success and power. The nation was secure and feared by her neighbors. David had the leisure even to build for himself a fine house. He was walking on the roof of it one day when he saw, in the garden of the house opposite, a woman at her bath. It was Bethsabee, and David was stricken with desire. He summoned her to the palace and committed adultery with her. After a time, Bethsabee sent word to David that she was with child.

Bethsabee's husband was Urias, a captain in David's army. He was in the field at the time, fighting the Ammonites. David had to find a way to conceal his paternity of Bethsabee's child. He finally settled upon a plan. He gave orders to Joab, commander in chief, that Urias be put into the forefront of a rash attack, and there abandoned. So it was done. The Hittite captain— for Urias was not even a Jew—died thinking his death the final pledge of loyalty to his king; he did not suspect that it was murder.

There came to the palace one day after all this a man of God, Nathan by name. With a sort of divine disregard for the niceties of courtly procedure he entered the chambers of the king, stood before him, and began to tell a story.

He told the story of two men, one exceedingly affluent, possessing cattle and land in great quantity, the other a poor farmer, a man who had a single joy in life, a lamb which he had bought with careful economy and which he treasured and took into his house.

One day, so ran Nathan's story, a guest stopped unexpectedly at the rich man's house. Hospitality required a dinner on such occasions, a rather nice dinner, too. But the rich man, instead of choosing the main course from among his countless flocks and herds, sent secretly to the house of his poor neighbor. He stole his lamb and with this made dinner for his guest.

When David heard the parable—for he realized that Nathan's story hid an application to someone and to some thing in the realm—he rose from his seat in great anger. He threatened severe punishment upon whoever in his kingdom had done such a thing. The prophet looked the king in the eye. *And Nathan said to David, Thou art the man* (II Kings 12:6).

Do we try to comfort ourselves with the thought that this story is not meant for us? *We are of Abraham's breed, nobody ever enslaved us yet; what dost thou mean by saying, You shall become free? And Jesus answered them, Believe me when I tell you this; everyone who acts sinfully is the slave of sin* . . . (John 8:33-34).

In his first letter St. John describes the concupiscence within us according to its three characteristic forms: the concupiscence of the flesh, the concupiscence of the eyes, and the pride of life.

The terms are general ones. Concupiscence of the flesh makes us think most immediately of the sensual satisfactions we crave and of the pampering care we constantly give our bodies. This becomes an especially virulent culture of sin when we associate others in this sensual satisfaction and use them as though they were instruments for our pleasure. It need not be merely sexual pampering. There is something of this domineering subjection of others to the interests of self in the case of the driver for whom politeness on the highway is a completely foreign idiom. It occurs in our behavior towards waitresses and delivery men, when we treat them like clumsy and inefficient vending machines, as though, by taking a salaried service job, they had lost somehow all right to our charity. *Right* to it, we must insist.

The temptation to reduce the human person to the level of a thing is a great one. It poisons the atmosphere of home. It turns the place of our job into a jungle. It reduces us who yield to it to an almost animal state, for it means that we accept the law of animal nature as our guiding principle: survival of the fittest. This is really what concupiscence of the flesh is: the tendency to make others the instruments of our own pleasure, to make our climb upward by stepping on their shoulders, to treat persons as though they were things.

The concupiscence of the eyes tends to take a reverse course. It leads us to flatter things with the identification of ourselves, to merge our persons with them. We give them a status which they do not have of their own and which they could not possibly merit. We make of ourselves a commodity on the market, selling ourselves, presenting ourselves as the first of the packages in which the product is offered to the public. We purchase things, beyond our means, not because we need them, not even

because we have use of them, but simply in order to have
them. Consuming goods has become an end in its own
right, apparently. It is a creed which retailers fervently
encourage.

This is an adult edition of something already present
in childhood. We have all seen it happen. Two children
are playing on the rug. One of the children is a visitor.
Toys are scattered all around. They belong to the child of
the house. The visitor reaches out for one of them. The
other child was not playing with it, but he immediately
raises a ruckus over it. Because he suddenly wants to
play with it? No, but because it is his, it is in fact himself;
he feels insecure when it is taken over to the uses of a
stranger.

The urge to possess is a good thing, for each man craves
security and the peaceful conditions of development for
his family and for himself. It is a good, but not a final
thing. The only final thing under God is the human
person. He is the only absolute within his universe. He
must not think that he can raise things to his level. The
concupiscence of the eyes tends to make us treat things
as though they were our own persons.

The third of St. John's root abnormalities in man's
moral life is called by him the pride of life. It is probably the fault we have in greatest degree and the one
we least suspect. We are condemned to an eternal prejudice in our own favor. We cannot escape it. That is not
the point. No one asks us to think that we can, by dint

of ascetic striving, rid ourselves of this prejudice. The point is to recognize that it is there and to draw the conclusion: we may, after all, be wrong. In spite of all, we may be wrong and the others right.

Certainly somewhere under this heading should be included the ability to apologize. One who knows how to say "I'm sorry" is not likely to grow apace in thinking that he is God. And that is what is odd: he *is* like God. The humble man *is* like God. And yet he does not fall into the trap of thinking so.

The pride of life lies deep in our natures. It is too ugly a thing to show its face quite plainly. It adopts myriad disguises before it finally comes to the surface. These masks, however, show, all of them, a common tendency: the individual tends to treat himself—his interests, his opinions, his plans—as though he were God.

Here, then, is the summary of the moral legacy of Adam: we, his children, tend to treat persons as though they were things, things as though they were ourselves, and ourselves as though we were God. That is concupiscence, in Paul's sense of the word; it is the death that is inside us, working itself out into our world.

Perhaps, like humility, recognition of our sinfulness is one of the last virtues to come to us, and if we do not live long enough, it may never come at all. Age and wisdom bring it and humility in tow. But recognition of our sinfulness, one way or another, either expressly or in figure and in image, is indispensable to any Christian life.

Since most of us were baptized as children, we have
not probably adverted to the fact that sorrow for sin,
at least in the person old enough to have committed
actual sin, is one of the conditions for the fruitful recep-
tion of the sacrament of Baptism. Without this contri-
tion, the character of Baptism, incorporating us into
the kingdom, would be given, but the grace of the
sacrament would be deferred until true sorrow was present. In the early centuries of the Church, when the
accent in the sacrament of Penance lay upon public confession and public reintegration into the community of
the faithful, the penitents were obliged to mingle with
the crowd of those not yet received into the Church, the
catechumens. On the day of receiving absolution, during
the last days of Holy Week, the penitents came with the
catechumens to the church. The bishop came down
among them. He addressed the penitents in particular
and set them apart, thus leading them away from their
association with the catechumens and restoring them to
their former places in the praying community. The
connection then between Baptism and Penance was clear.
The Fathers of the Church could speak of these two
sacraments as two planks of salvation held out to those
who had met shipwreck.

Baptism is already, in fact, a foreshadowing of the
sacrament of Penance. Even if we have no personal sins,
even if our minds have not reached a state mature enough
to formulate the psalmist's cry—*For indeed, I was born*

in sin; guilt was with me already when my mother conceived me (Ps. 50:7) — yet the actions of Baptism and the prayers accompanying them convey the essential meaning, that admission of one's sinfulness is the condition for entry into the kingdom of God.

These rites say something else as well, something perhaps even more fundamental.

It is that only grace can tell us what sin is.

Ordinarily we have no difficulty in cataloguing the evils of the world. We have visited the children's ward of large hospitals and have come away shaken to the furthest corners of our being. We remember the classmate who drowned. We remember the shrunken figures imbedded in the wet sands of Omaha Beach and their epitaph muttered by an English officer: "Brave men, brave men." The list of evils is long, automatic on our lips.

How many of us, in drawing it up, would have included sin?

Strange and terrible victory of Satan, this fogging of our minds, this vigorous sensitivity to what hurts man and dull complacency in what hurts God.

Of course, it is not as though Satan did not have something to build upon. We do not really know, after all, who God is; how can we know what it means to offend him? Christ prayed from the cross, *Father, forgive them; they do not know what it is they are doing* (Luke 23:34). But none of us knows what it is that we do when we offend God and his Son. We must, however, try to find out, and only grace can teach us.

This is the lesson of the saints, who so often mention their sinfulness and die with a prayer for mercy on their lips. It is not that they are greater sinners than they think, but that God is yet more holy than they had dreamed. Grace revealed him to them more and more as he is. The saints have come closest to the vision of Isaias and have awakened to the immense holiness of God, in whose fires they see better their own condition as sinners.

Sin is a phenomenon of the supernatural order. It belongs to the sphere of divine charity and liberality. That is why it is a mystery. We can never come to the bottom of it. And only prayer can help us to begin our understanding of what it is.

This is why Holy Mother the Church has encouraged us to go to confession often, even if we do not have serious sin upon our soul. The proper grace of the sacrament of Penance is to reveal to us how much each of us stands in need of the mercy of God. Only grace can tell us that in any case, and the grace of confession tells us best of all.

What, after all, is the grand strategy of Satan?

He comes with a temptation to impurity, for example. There seems so much to excuse it. There is very little stigma attached. It is so terribly easy to do. It is certainly not the worst sin in the world. And then—Satan may not say this very loudly, but he says it all the same—one can always confess the sin.

So the bait is taken. Confession follows before very long, if this is a relatively new thing in the person's life. And lo! the sin is easy to confess, the priest is very understanding, and what is more, sorrow for the sin is sincere, noticeably sincere, satisfyingly sincere.

All the same, it is easier to sin the next time.

Something is happening here. Satan's strategy is at work. The number of sins grows greater and greater, the time between confessions longer and longer. One gets used to the habit of, not sinning merely, but remaining in the state of sin. The thought is no longer shocking. The skies have not fallen, nor have friends turned away, nor has the paycheck decreased. It becomes harder and harder to be sorry for one's sin. A dullness and insensitivity has begun to jell. The appeals of grace sound farther and farther away. Suddenly, when the time is ripe, the word "hypocrite" falls upon the consciousness like heavy chains upon the street. It suddenly seems an heroic and manly thing *not* to go to confession.

Satan's joy is complete. He has through repeated sins induced what to him was far more interesting than sin, a heavy dullness to the appeals of grace. He has tied up the bundle neatly with a knotty question of motives, which hardly any individual is capable of solving for himself, and made the very solution of this question im-

possible by demanding apparently that it be solved outside the conditions where alone a solution can be had,
the conditions of grace, namely, and of the sacrament. It
is not mere dealing in subtleties to point out that one
goes to hell, not exactly for mortal sin, but for per-
severance in it until the end.

And so it happens that even the lucky man, the man
taken, for example, on emergency into the Catholic
hospital, the man with family saying the rosary for him
and sisters and nurses hovering about him, the man put
into a room with a fellow member of the Church who
perhaps receives Communion every morning, the man
who lies in bed and sees the crucifix upon the wall—it
often happens that such a man, fully conscious of his
danger, can tell the priest when he comes to offer confession, "Oh, Father, some other time." Every pastor and
hospital chaplain can recount dozens of such cases.

That is Satan's final triumph, to get his victim into
such a state of insensitivity to grace that all the spiritual
help in the world would not change him. Do we remember the story of the rich man in hell?

> Whereupon he said, Then, father, I pray thee send
> him to my own father's house; for I have five brethren;
> let him give these a warning, so that they may not come,
> in their turn, into this place of suffering.
>
> Abraham said to him, They have Moses and the
> prophets; let them listen to these.

They will not do that, father Abraham, said he; but if a messenger comes to them from the dead, they will repent.

But he answered him, If they do not listen to Moses and the prophets, they will be unbelieving still, though one should rise from the dead. (Luke 16:27-31)

Admission of our sinfulness is not only one of the conditions for entry into the kingdom, it is also one of the conditions for staying in it, once there. Our capacity for sorrow is one of the surest signs of spiritual health. Confession is the gauge of it.

To those who complained that he sat down to table with publicans and sinners, Jesus said, *It is not those who are in health that have need of a physician, it is those who are sick. I have come to call sinners, not the just* (Mark 2:17). But as Msgr. Guardini has pointed out in his book, *The Lord,* we are all of us sinners. Christ died for all. If we do not think of ourselves as sinners, it is only because Satan has in our case gone further along in his strategy than we suspect.

The publican and the Pharisee went one day to the temple to pray. The Pharisee advanced to the front and, standing, told God of his accomplishments and fidelities above those of the ordinary run of men. But the publican remained in the rear. He beat his breast and prayed, *O God, be merciful to me a sinner.* He was right. He was a sinner. He was a tax gatherer for the hated Roman power. More likely than not, he was an extortioner and oppressor of the poor.

Only, he admitted it, and he was the one who went away justified in God's sight.

5. *The Sign of the Cross*

St. John says that God is love, and in another place he completes this thought by adding, *God so loved the world, that he gave up his only-begotten Son* . . . (John 3:16).

To say love alone leaves in obscurity the chief aspect of God's love for man: that it is long-suffering, patient, faithful. That it is not merely over and beyond but even against the merits of man. The love of God is above all merciful.

> If the Lord has held you closely to him and shewed you special favor, it was not that you overshadowed other peoples in greatness; of all nations you are the smallest. No, it was because the Lord loved you. . . . (Deut. 7:7-8)

And when the heap of Israel's sins blotted practically all else from sight,

What, can a woman forget her child that is still un-
weaned, pity no longer the son she bore in her womb?
Let her forget; I will not be forgetful of thee. (Is. 49:15)

It takes a strong love to be merciful. Moses might be
carried away in an excess of discouraged anger, but God
is patient, and inscribes the tablets of stone all over again.
God's love is the strongest of all love. That is why it can
afford to be most merciful.

Of course, we do not know *why* God should so love
man. We know *that* it is so, and it startles us.

What was the state of man before the Son of God
came into the world?

Man was the victim and the slave of sin, of Satan, of
death—held in bondage under a reign of death, weighed
down by a body of death, completely at a loss to do anything about it. Even the Law, the privileged dispensation
of God's will for him, became the cataloguing of his
faults rather than of his successes. Man breathed lethal
airs. There was no healthy shore to which he could
escape.

None of this was unforeseen.

In the fullness of time the Word, though equal to the
Father and true God himself, emptied himself. He took
on the shape of man, the *nature of a slave* which man was
(Phil. 2:7). He was fashioned in the likeness of man, he
presented himself to man in thoroughly human form,
born of a woman, and obedient.

The Son of God entered into this place of death, which was our natural habitat. That is what St. Paul means when he says that God made his Son *sin* for our sakes— *Christ never knew sin, but God made him into sin for us*—that is, the Son of God entered into the abode of sin, the atmosphere, the field of force where sin was at work, and spared himself nothing of all the pain and sorrows which are the visible signs of sin in the world. That is the reason Jesus loved to speak of himself as the Son of Man: he came to subject himself to man's lot.

Satan had tempted Adam and Eve in the garden with the dream of becoming like God. Strange to say, the dream was to be more than idle wishing. Satan knew it. That was his astuteness. He took a fact and distorted it. It would be a fact that man would become like God, but not because man would lift himself up to God's level. God would rather bend himself down to man's. *Christ never knew sin, and God made him into sin for us, so that in him we might be turned into the holiness of God* (II Cor. 5:21).

What was Jesus' work as man to be?

Our redemption might have been worked out quickly and easily. The Incarnation was not absolutely necessary. Even after it took place, there was no essential need to go to the lengths the gospels tell us of. A single cry of the babe lying on his mother's arm would have been enough, or even no pain or suffering at all but only the barest human gesture, of recognition, for example, or request.

God knew that the evil was too deep in us to be cured by such facile means. It had been too long with us. It lay snugly upon us like an old familiar bathrobe. It was a shabby thing, but we felt comfortable in it. We were used to it. We would not change lightly, not without a jolt.

Then there was another thing. Those who are the image of God cannot be herded back to their maker like cattle back to the enclosure. Man was the translation of God's freedom into finite terms. Besides, there was good left in the world and in Adam after the fall. God's intention was to repair, not to make over entirely. He would fan into flame the remaining spark of man's dignity, and he would give man a share in doing it.

This Jesus whom our eyes have gazed upon and our hands touched, who was in the beginning—*the Word,* who is life (I John 1:1)—this Jesus is God's reparation in the world—and man's—working not from a distance but up close, immersed into man's world. God enters history in order to repair it from within. God became the Son of Man.

In doing this Jesus would repeat as it were the whole history of the relationship between God and man. He would in his own person and lifetime recapitulate the gestures of man to God. He would be a sort of lineman, tracing back along the wires to find the root cause of all the trouble. And he would do it, not from any merely human desire to imitate God's past heroes, but because he was conscious of the fact that the whole burden of the Law and the Prophets rested upon his person.

Jesus was prophet. The people thought of him in these terms (Matt. 16:14). They compared him to the prophets of old—Elias, for example, or Jeremias. They contrasted him with the other rabbinic teachers of Judaism, *And they were amazed by his teaching, for he sat there teaching them like one who had authority, not like the scribes* (Mark 1:22).

More important, Jesus claimed this title as his own, and claimed it in a way which left no doubt at all about the unique prerogatives which the title included in his person. In the Sermon on the Mount Jesus used the formula which must have struck the Jew of that day like a thunderbolt: *You have heard that it was said to the men of old ... but I tell you....* The formula occurs three solemn times, Matthew 5:21,27,33. Jesus was recapitulating in himself all those prophets who had gone before him, but this time in a manner which they could never approach.

And what happened?

The terrible sin of the Pharisees was to deny the Spirit which spoke so plainly to their ears in the accents of Jesus. They said that it was not God's Spirit, the Spirit of prophecy, which inhabited him, but Satan. This deliberate blinding was the unforgivable sin. When they baited him, Jesus answered:

As for your father Abraham, his heart was proud to see the day of my coming; he saw, and rejoiced to see it.

Then the Jews asked him, Hast thou seen Abraham, thou, who art not yet fifty years old?

And Jesus said to them, Believe me, before ever Abraham came to be, I am. (John 8:56-58)

There was much more than mere continuity between Jesus and the prophets. Now God spoke in his Son (Heb. 1:2). The wonderful thing is that in his Son man also spoke and gave testimony to the glory of God.

Only, speaking is not enough.

Jesus was king. He had received the anointing of his father David, and an even more precious throne had been promised him. How make the people understand? They wanted Jesus their king, but in their own way, not God's. It was not really the Jews who came nearest to understanding, it was Pilate. He confronted Jesus as the representative of the pagan world, already half conscious of its need for redemption.

So Pilate went back into the palace, and summoned Jesus; Art thou king of the Jews? he asked. . . .

My kingdom, said Jesus, does not belong to this world. If my kingdom were one which belonged to this world, my servants would be fighting, to prevent my falling into the hands of the Jews; but no, my kingdom does not take its origin here.

Thou art a king, then? Pilate asked.

And Jesus answered, It is thy own lips that have called me a king. What I was born for, what I came into the world for, is to bear witness of the truth. Whoever belongs to the truth listens to my voice. (John 18:33, 36-37)

Pilate could not understand the sort of kingdom which was not of this world. And neither could the Jews. Sometimes neither can we.

Because he was king, Jesus was not a man merely as other men are. He was a man as Adam was, a representative. He could speak for a whole people. He could sum up in himself the allegiance of a people, more than Moses or Samuel or even David could ever have hoped to do.

That is why Jesus was, like Adam, the object of Satan's particular attention. The stakes were supremely important. This was the second Adam, and Satan knew it.

Jesus was prophet and king.

Most of all, Jesus was priest.

We have to keep in mind two facts. In Christ dwelt the fullness of grace and truth; Jesus was the holiness of God living, walking, teaching among men. That is the first fact. But the world was not a neutral thing in his path, passively disposed to accept him. On the contrary, it was actively hostile. It did not want to be taught. Even his own received him not. That is the second fact.

Unless one sees the satanic backdrop against which every deed of Jesus is performed, it is impossible to understand anything of his life. He was the first to wage total war against *princedoms and powers,* against *those who have mastery of the world in these dark days . . . malign influences in an order higher than ours* (Eph. 6:12). Angel choirs may have heralded Christ's birth, but the scene of Bethlehem was marked by a frantic flight as well, and by the murder of the Innocents. A dark angel was present there. Already he let it be known that there could be only one issue from the confrontation of Christ and the world.

That is why Jesus is a priest, that is to say, one who sacrifices.

It is also why the victim would be himself.

The inaugural act of our Lord's public ministry was his baptism in the Jordan by St. John. Looking back upon it now with the understanding of the Scriptures which we have in Christ's Spirit, we can see that even at that early moment the final issue of Jesus' work was announced. It is a point which has particular reference to us who are trying to relive consciously the transforming force of our baptism.

For as John poured the water over our Lord's brow the heavens opened up. The Spirit of God descended upon him in the form of a dove and a heavenly voice was heard: *This is my beloved son, in whom I am well pleased* (Matt. 3:17).

These words are a citation of the first verse of the forty-second chapter of the prophet Isaias. Now this is the first of those sections in Isaias' prophecy which have since come to be known as the Songs of the Suffering Servant of God.

Jesus' baptism therefore is already the public statement that he is the new representative of the human race:

> Thus says the Lord God . . . True to my purpose, I, the Lord, have summoned thee, taking thee by the hand and protecting thee, to make, through thee, a covenant with my own people, to shed, through thee, light over the Gentiles: to give sight to blinded eyes, to set the prisoner free from his captivity, from the dungeon where he lies in darkness. (Is. 42:5-7)

It is also clear what will be the issue of his work, for the fifty-third chapter of the same prophet explains further:

> This servant of his will appear among us, unregarded as brushwood shoot, as a plant in waterless soil; no stateliness here, no majesty, no beauty, as we gaze upon him, to win our hearts. Nay, here is one despised, left out of all human reckoning; bowed with misery, and no stranger to weakness. . . . (Is. 53:2-3)

This answers the question why Jesus, who was sinless, should be baptized. His baptism was the annunciation of that other baptism which would be in blood on the cross. Others had come to John to be baptized for their own sins; Jesus came to announce his baptism for the sins of others. The scene on the banks of the Jordan was a foreshadowing of another scene on the hill of Golgotha. Hence Jesus could say, *There is a baptism I must needs be baptized with, and how impatient am I for its accomplishment* (Luke 12:50). His death would be a general baptism for all men. The waters which flowed from his pierced side would infuse our fonts with life.

When that day came Jesus would have traveled the course of man's dealings with God back to their starting-point. He would be where only one other had been before him. And he would be alone.

Shortly before the decisive Pasch the chief priests had been afraid to arrest Jesus because they feared the people, who looked upon him as a prophet. But the night preceding Good Friday they were afraid no longer. They even got one of his followers to betray him.

A few days earlier, the people had welcomed Jesus into the city with hosannas for the king, the son of David. Now the agents of the temple find no difficulty in inciting them to cry out for the release of a murderer and a thief, instead of Jesus, whom they are ready to crucify.

How rapidly things changed, those last hours. Jesus sat down to table with the twelve. Soon there were only eleven. He went with these into the garden and took aside three for his encouragement and consolation. Their eyes were heavy, and, besides, they could not really understand what was happening. After a time the chief priests and temple guards came up and arrested him. *And now all his disciples abandoned him, and fled* (Matt. 26:56). Jesus went in to his Passion alone, with nothing left, apparently, of his prerogatives as prophet and king—with none, at least, of their temporal accompaniments. He faced his tormentors only with that nature which was given him with the title he loved so well, Son of Man. He was the second Adam.

It had been in the garden that Adam had failed mankind, so it was in a garden that Jesus faced those into whom Satan had entered. There he accepted the challenge of the hour which belonged to the powers of darkness.

As it was by a tree that Adam had failed, so it was on a tree that Jesus gained for us re-entry into life.

As Adam had slept and God from his side had drawn the woman who would, unhappily, be the occasion of man's sin, now in saving contrast Jesus bowed his head in death and from his side, as the Fathers of the Church love to repeat, his spouse, the Church, came forth; she would be the mother of divine life for all the people.

There was a legend current in the early Middle Ages that the cross had been planted above the very spot where Adam had been buried, and that the lower tip of the wood rested upon our first parent's skull. This gave rise to the custom of putting a skull and bones near the bottom of the vertical staff of our crucifixes. It too is a reminder that Jesus is the second Adam.

When we entered into the baptismal waters, we knew that we were entering into a place of withdrawal, of renunciation, of death.

But whose death?

Adam's? Yes, partly, for we carried with us the burden of his fault. Yet Adam's death could not revivify us.

Our own? In a way, for we too had ratified the sin of Adam within us. We had countersigned it. We had to dissolve that contract. But, we could not do it on our own.

The death in which we were immersed at baptism and which is the prelude of life for us is the death of Christ.

> You know well enough that we who were taken up into Christ by baptism have been taken up, all of us, into his death. In our baptism, we have been buried with him, died like him, that so, just as Christ was raised up by his Father's power from the dead, we too might live and move in a new kind of existence. . . .

> And if we have died with Christ, we have faith to believe that we shall share his life. We know that Christ, now he has risen from the dead, cannot die any more; death has no more power over him; the death he died was a death, once for all, to sin; the life he now lives is a life that looks towards God. And you, too, must think of yourselves as dead to sin, and alive with a life that looks towards God, through Christ Jesus our Lord. (Rom. 6:3-4, 8-11)

It is for these reasons that the Church has never permitted herself to approach these scenes of her Lord's suffering in a state of pathetic and helpless despondency.

Like Mary she *stands* beneath the cross. On Holy Saturday night, when the new Christians are to be received through baptism into the Church, she clothes herself, not in mourning but in white joyous vestments; she cries out, not in pain but in song:

> without redemption life itself had been no boon! How wonderful the condescension of thy mercy towards us; how far beyond all reckoning thy loving kindness! To ransom thy slave, thou gavest up thy Son! O truly necessary sin of Adam, that Christ's death blotted out! O happy fault, that merited such a redeemer!

In each Mass she repeats with tender gratitude, ". . . mindful of thy most blessed passion. . . ." *Blessed* passion! The word which she applies to the saints after their triumph, when all opposition has been finally overcome!

Our baptism is not a making the best out of a bad deal. We are more privileged than Adam, far more.

> It was through one man that guilt came into the world; and, since death came owing to guilt, death was handed on to all mankind by one man. . . . In this, Adam was the type of him who was to come. Only, the grace which came to us was out of all proportion to the fault. If this one man's fault brought death on a whole multitude, all the more lavish was God's grace, shewn to a whole multitude, that free gift he made us in the grace brought by one man, Jesus Christ. (Rom. 5:12, 14-15)

6. *The Lord's Mark*

And now, here is a message from the Lord to Jacob, his creature, to the Israel he fashioned: Do not be afraid, I have bought thee for myself, and given thee the name thou bearest: thou belongest to me. Pass through water, and I will be with thee, so that the flood shall not drown thee; walk amid the flames, and thou shalt not be burnt, the fire shall have no power to catch thee. I am the Lord thy God, the Holy One of Israel, thy deliverer. (Is. 43:1-3)

If someone asks us why we are Catholics, our first answer can only be: Because God has chosen us. Just as God chose to create us and then to redeem us, so he has chosen, even prior to any consideration of our own merits, to bring us into his kingdom. It is a kingdom with a long history.

Abraham was the first one chosen by God as, not a member, merely, but the father of the kingdom. God

promised him that he would be the ancestor of a great
people. God made a pact with Abraham. If the people
proved obedient and loyal to this alliance, they would
prosper and become mighty before all nations.

But as Abraham's clan grew, and especially as the
Israelites became powerful and entered as equals upon
treaties with neighboring pagan countries, jealousies and
dissensions appeared. There was a jockeying for favored
positions. The kingdom itself was split. Some Hebrews
found more in common with their rich pagan friends
than with their poor Jewish compatriots. Marriages between Jew and pagan took place. Pagan customs crept
into the rites which God had established. Soon it became
evident that the members of the kingdom of God were
no longer all those who could claim physical descent
from Abraham, but only a few from among them, those
still loyal to all the terms of the pact God had made with
his people.

Unfortunately, as defeat followed upon defeat, even
these few became scattered and discouraged. There were
not many true sons of Abraham left when Christ was
born. We have seen how, even during his own lifetime,
the number of those who were loyal to him until the
end declined steadily. All the apostles fled when Jesus
was arrested. It is true, Mary, some of the holy women,
and John were there at the foot of the cross. But, in a
deeper sense, even their loyalty depended upon what
Jesus did and what only Jesus could do at that terrible

moment when the entire kingdom of God was compressed into himself alone. Because he was God, an incommunicable primacy put him beyond the reach of any creature. Because he was so thoroughly man, he experienced even that sense of dereliction which man has when he is led somehow to think that God, too, has abandoned him to his fate.

But when Jesus uttered his final cry and died, a Roman soldier, reflecting on all that had happened, was moved to testify, *No doubt but this was the son of God* (Mark 15:39). This soldier may be called the first convert. The kingdom in him began to grow populous again. The Church had begun its march across the globe.

Perhaps we are moving too quickly if we call the Roman soldier the first convert; the only real entry into the kingdom is by way of Baptism. Jesus left no doubt about that. Man must be born anew through the administering of water and the Holy Spirit. The incorporation into Christ's kingdom is by physical means. These in their turn put a stamp upon the baptized as followers of Christ. In theological language this stamp is called the character of the sacrament; it is conferred in the three sacraments of Baptism, Confirmation and Holy Orders. It is a spiritual mark, very real, the signature of God upon our souls in proof of our being followers of his Son. To explain something of the nature of this mark is also to explain what it means to be a citizen of Christ's kingdom.

In the baptismal waters we come into contact with the death and resurrection of Jesus. Something objective happens to us. It is not an idle meeting, from which we walk away unchanged. We are, literally, marked men.

We had borne within us, as children of Adam, the mark of his lineage. Becoming children of God in Christ we were marked interiorly as his. The circumcision had been the foreshadowing of this future belonging. The comparison of Baptism to circumcision was made by St. Paul, but he points out that the sacrament makes us much more the children of God, his chosen people, because our allegiance is inscribed interiorly in the heart instead of in the flesh.

Paul's word for this mark was "a sealing," or "an anointing." The Fathers of the Church used the same phraseology. They compared it to the brand denoting ownership burnt upon animals, or to the image impressed upon a coin, and most often of all to the tattoo which professional soldiers bore as badges of their allegiance. This last was an especially significant figure, for the soldiers' tattoo denoted not merely allegiance but also function and was, furthermore, indelible.

This sealing and branding is accomplished in Baptism, which is the first application to us of the merits of Christ. It marks us as belonging to Christ, before even we have begun to use the privileges of grace which this belonging implies.

No commitment of one's life should be lightly volunteered, and the commitment of Baptism least of all. St. Cyril, in fourth century Jerusalem, used to admonish his catechumens:

> This is in truth a serious matter, brethren, and you must approach it solemnly. You are, each of you, on the point of being presented to God, before innumerable hosts of angels; the Holy Ghost is on the point of setting a seal on your souls; you are coming for enlistment under the great king. Make ready, therefore. (Catechesis III: 3-4) [1]

It was especially St. Augustine who gave clarity to the doctrine of the sacramental character as it was handed down from the New Testament through the Fathers. He gave it that expressive, comprehensive title: "the Lord's mark." What does it mean to say that we bear the Lord's mark?

We have seen that when St. Paul speaks of our inheritance in Adam's sin, he speaks not merely of the original sin within us but also of our immersion in some sort of atmosphere, which is rather difficult to describe, but which for St. Paul is quite real: it is a malignant force operative in the world, a burden upon us, a "sense of sin," a polluted air we breathe, a place of death. It is a highly localized thing, and it is operative. It reminds us of those areas of the world where a particular disease

---

[1] Quoted from Bernard Leeming, S.J., *Principles of Sacramental Theology* (Westminster, Newman, 1956).

seems to be prevalent because of some strange combination of climate, nourishment, and cultural heritage.

When, therefore, St. Paul tells of our leaving this place where sin is endemic and of our beginning to live *in Christ*, as he often phrased it, he stresses our beginning to live in a new kind of atmosphere, with a new and stronger kind of life. Through us the grace of Christ is let loose into the world. It goes where we go. We, the citizens of the kingdom, constitute the place, the field of it.

> Remember, then, what you once were. . . . In those days there was no Christ for you; you were outlaws from the commonwealth of Israel, strangers to every covenant, with no promise to hope for, with the world about you, and no God. But now you are in Christ Jesus; now, through the blood of Christ, you have been brought close, you who were once so far away. . . .

> You are no longer exiles, then, or aliens; the saints are your fellow-citizens, you belong to God's household. Apostles and prophets are the foundation on which you were built, and the chief corner-stone of it is Jesus Christ himself. In him the whole fabric is bound together, as it grows into a temple, dedicated to the Lord; in him you too are being built in with the rest, so that God may find in you a dwelling-place for his Spirit. (Eph. 2:11-14, 19-22)

It is unfortunate that the words *laity, layman* have taken in our time so pale a color and so dry a sound. The words are used by professional people to designate one whose knowledge of their field is in its infancy and probably rather superficial. They have become profane words, and not very flattering ones at that.

In reality the words laity and laymen are first of all religious terms. They derive from the Greek *laos,* which was the word consistently used in the Greek translation of the Hebrew scriptures to designate the people of God. It is a lofty title. It goes back to the first comings of God into history when he formed for himself a people and gave them their dignity in these terms: *You shall be my people* [laos], *and I will be Your God* (Ezec. 36:28). Those who receive Baptism and the baptismal character are the heirs of that promise. St. Peter writes to them and tells them what the word laity really means:

> You are a chosen race, a royal priesthood, a consecrated nation, a people God means to have for himself; it is yours to proclaim the exploits of the God who has called you out of darkness into his marvellous light. Time was when you were not a people at all, now you are God's people. . . . (I Peter 2:9-10)

Who before this *were not a people!* How true that is, for sin was the principle of disunity among us.

But even now—and here is an important point—sin is not absent from us, even after our becoming members of the kingdom. How can we be said to be a holy people, one dedicated to God, if we are still sinners?

It is especially here that the doctrine of the baptismal character is most expressive. It helps us to understand what exactly is meant by the word *holy*.

Over the centuries, the word has come to mean an heroic fidelity to the commandments and to grace. This is not, of course, a false meaning, but it is not the meaning which the prophets, St. Paul, and the Fathers of the Church had primarily in mind when they called the people holy. For them, the first meaning of *holy* was not "sinless" but rather "consecrated," that is, set apart for God, reserved to him, taken from the claim of man. It was God who did this; the initiative was always his.

For St. Paul, all the baptized were holy. He addressed the Christians of Rome as the well-beloved of God . . . saints by their calling (Rom. 1:7), though he knew well enough that there were sinners among them. He wrote to the Corinthians as the *sanctified in Christ Jesus . . . called to be holy* (I Cor. 1:2), though the letter goes on to criticize them severely for their failure to punish the incestuous and rebellious persons in their midst and for their allowing the Lord's supper to degenerate into a display of greediness and even drunkenness. Such sins as these exclude the grace of justification (I Cor. 5:11-13; 6:9-11; 11:18-32), but they do not dissolve the Lord's mark, the badge of incorporation into the holy people. That remains in spite of the sin.

The basic reason for the indelibility of the baptismal character is at the same time the fundamental aspect in the meaning of the word holy. The reason is this: in this setting apart for God's service and use, the initiative is always with God. It is a calling man has received, above and beyond his merits for such a thing, and, as his actions are not the primary consideration in the granting of membership in God's kingdom, so, too, man's acts will not be factors which will remove the mark which God has put upon him, branding him as God's own.

This element of passivity in our Christian calling helps us to understand why the Church has long had the tradition of baptizing children and others incapable of speaking an allegiance for themselves. Even in the case of the adult—though, obviously, more is required of him by way of faith and intention than in the case of the child —even in this case there is in Baptism the ritual expression of the fact that God is choosing him, that the initiative lies with God, that a stamp is being put upon the soul which only he can put there. It is the seal of his ring. No other wears it. *That love resides, not in our shewing any love for God, but in his shewing love for us first, when he sent out his Son to be an atonement for our sins* (I John 4:10).

This badge of belonging can be contradicted. It can be frustrated and allowed through desuetude to vanish from consciousness, but it cannot be lost. The baptized who commits sin commits a more awful sin than the non-baptized who yields with equal deliberation to the same objective fault. The baptized is a member of the household of God. He hurts, when he sins, the members of the family, not some vague "other" with whom he has no special ties. The baptized who strays from the duties of his faith is not booked on the angel's docket as a vagrant, but as a deserter. One does not escape from Christ, once he bears his seal.

The Lord's mark is furthermore an active thing. The kingdom in which the baptismal character enlists us is a missionary kingdom. Its citizens have not received participation in the vivifying atmosphere of Christ's life as a treasure to hoard or bury in the ground. As the kingdom is missionary, so are the individuals making it up, so is the sign and character which marks them followers of Christ. One does not escape either from Christ or from the Christian job.

How exactly is this force qualified in us?

St. Paul writes that we are *grafted* onto Christ. The word is too expressive to allow for some sort of vague and formless participation. Christ was king, prophet, priest. So, in our measure, are we. His virtue flows in us and he now rules his kingdom, instructs his people, offers his sacrifice through the members of the Church who prolong him in the world.

Such a participation is not grace itself. A person can be baptized and yet, through impenitence, be incapable of receiving the baptismal grace. This will come, however, when sorrow comes, for the seal of the Lord is a dynamic participation in Christ, which with all its being calls for its complement in grace. One who has the baptismal character and yet does not live the baptismal life is, religiously at least, in a state of violent contradiction. He has become supernaturally schizoid. There is a dispersion present in his soul, and it will in time blossom into a luxuriant chaos in his life.

The baptismal character looks forward in another way. It looks forward to the characters of the sacrament of Confirmation and of Holy Orders. It may be spoken of as being already these further qualifications in their initial stages. Both Confirmation and Holy Orders come as the crowning of a tendency and dynamism which Baptism has implanted. This does not say that they are not real additions. They are. But they are not discontinuous additions. The line is one, though spliced. For this reason it is not metaphor to speak of the priesthood of the laity. Something of the priest is present in the baptized. It appears as an eligibility and even a sort of deeply planted desire to exercise within the Church the function of him who sacrifices. We will return to this topic in the chapter on the Mass of the People.

This is the point which must be ever before our eyes when thinking of our incorporation into the body of Christ, his Church, and of the baptismal character which is the initial badge of that allegiance. We are in the Church as members charged with a function. We live in an atmosphere bathed in grace—*All you who have been baptized in Christ's name have put on the person of Christ* (Gal. 3:27)—but not as though it were a shelter, rather as though it were a field of force which both activates and directs us.

We become marked men in order to turn back towards that atmosphere of sin in which we once lived. Only now the situation is different. The world around us may seem to remain the same. In fact, it is the same. But *we* are not. *We* have changed. Something ontological and irrevocable has happened to us. Our grafting into Christ is a physical thing which channels Christ's life into our activity. An intrinsic thing, not a word spoken from afar, nor a merely moral union such as binds the partners of a contract. Christ is not a partner to us. He is the vine, and we are the branches.

This is what we wanted. We knew all along, when considering the nature of sin, that what we needed was not a change of circumstances but a change of heart. Now, this change has really been brought about.

Certainly, the world is no less hostile than it was. To meet it will mean to transform it or to be transformed— to suffer, consequently, and, perhaps, to die. But we needn't be afraid, we who are now the members of his little flock. He who took the initiative to redeem us, to bring us into his body the Church and to set his mark upon us, knows who are his. We are individuals for him, not paper members of his kingdom or mere digits in a long arithmetical line. God calls us by our first name. We can never be anything other than an individual for him, someone who never existed before nor will ever exist again afterwards—someone unique in all creation. We are priceless to him.

> I have bartered away Egypt to win thee, Ethiopia and Saba for thy ransom. So prized, so honoured, so dearly loved, that I am ready to give up mankind in thy place, a world to save thee. Do not be afraid, I am with thee.
> (Is. 43:3-5)

It should be a source of immense comfort to us that the value God places on our persons is not measured by our love but by his.

Confirmation

7. *First Names*

The sacrament of Confirmation is the fulfillment of the sacrament of Baptism just as the mission of the Holy Spirit is the fulfillment of the coming of Christ. And just as the Holy Spirit is, as St. Paul often says, Christ's Spirit, so the grace of Confirmation is Baptism's grace perfected and completed for a new need and a new role. In the early Church the two sacraments were given one immediately following the other, thus marking the natural progression between them. In the Eastern Church the practice still holds true.

Confirmation is called the sacrament of the Holy Spirit. Of course, the Holy Spirit was already given in Baptism. There is no incorporation into Christ except through him who is the Spirit of Jesus and "the soul of the Mystical Body" (Pope Pius XII, *Mystici Corporis*). Yet something special is done.

In general, the special grace of Confirmation is the

strengthening of the Christian in the dignity which Baptism has given him. St. Cyril of Jerusalem put it to his catechumens in this way:

> Just as Jesus, after his Baptism and the descent of the Holy Ghost upon him, went out to meet his enemy, so, too, after Baptism and the ineffable anointing, protected by the panoply of the Holy Spirit, do you hold yourself firm against all inimical power. (Catechesis 21,4)

Confirmation is a step to which Baptism quite normally leads, because what we have professed in Baptism is not so much a doctrine, a set of beliefs—though we have done that—but a way of life and a person. That means activity and reaction on our part.

In a sense we were passive in Baptism. Something was done to us. A status was given to us. But this status entails a function, and it is for the sake of this function that the sacrament of Confirmation comes with its strengthening power. The function has two aspects, one which is internal and one which is external, one which is individual and refers to the saving of one's own soul, and one which is social and refers to the salvation of others. This chapter takes up the first of those aspects, the next treats the second.

The first application of Christ's merits to our persons is the mark given us in Baptism, which makes us members of the kingdom. In itself this is not enough. Something only becomes truly our own—in the case of adults, at least—when we deliberately face it, recognize its presence and what it entails, and say, "All right, I want that. That's what I want to be." We saw that we had by our own actual sins ratified inside us the sin inherited from Adam. So, too, the stronger life of grace now given us must be ratified and put to work by our own deliberate decision. This is the only way to arrive at Christian maturity.

It is true, in another order of things God might have done without the ratification of man's free will, but for some reason the record of his dealings with man seems to be against such a possibility. God has always shown a remarkable degree of respect for man's freedom. He never wished to salvage man's nature uniquely in God's own act, not even in the sole act of Christ. Perhaps God was remembering that freedom is the chief of his own attributes, and that man is created in his image. This, at least, is how the French poet Charles Péguy saw the problem. He wrote, putting the words into God's mouth:

> When once you have known what it is to be loved
> freely, submission no longer has any taste.
>
> All the prostrations in the world
>
> Are not worth the beautiful upright attitude of a
> free man as he kneels. All the submission, all the
> dejection in the world
>
> Are not equal in value to the soaring up point,

The beautiful straight soaring up of one single in-
vocation

From a love that is free.[1]

The first effect of Confirmation is to help us freely say
—the sacrament does not say it *for* us—"I want to be
what I now am, a member of Christ's kingdom."

There is a passage in the New Testament which will
help us realize what this means.

One day, apparently towards the middle of his
ministry, Jesus was walking with his disciples to the city
of Caesarea Philippi, a new Roman town. He put a question to his disciples: *What do men say of the Son of Man?*
Who do they think he is? (Matt. 16:13).

Now, the people of those days and regions were aware
of a dimension behind such a question which is lost
upon us in these impersonal times. For them, the *name*
touched upon the secret wellsprings of a person's in-
dividuality. To ask about the name, to learn the name
of a person, was to ask about and to learn the very
essence which defined this individual in the eyes of God
and man. It was to ask, not about some conventional tag
tacked onto a citizen for the sake of avoiding mistakes,
but about what the person was. Hence the Jewish doctors
of the Law had the principle, "The person is the name,
the name is the person."

[1] Charles Péguy, "Freedom," *God Speaks*, trans. Julian Greene
(New York: Pantheon, 1945), p. 29.

This was the reason that the rabbinic doctors would not permit even the pronouncing of the name of God. This is the background of the commandment *Thou shalt not take the name of the Lord, thy God, in vain.* This is the source of that constant usage in the Bible and in the liturgy of such phrases as *In the name of.* . . . In St. Paul's letter to the Philippians there is a passage which brings all this out:

> . . . so that at the name of Jesus everyone in heaven, on earth, and beneath the earth should bend the knee and should publicly acknowledge to the glory of God the Father that Jesus Christ is THE LORD.[2]

An American Indian would understand all this easily, because he knows what it means to name someone Running Waters or Sleeping Bear. It may even help us to understand that sentence so oddly phrased by our Lady when she spoke to Bernadette, "Tell the bishop, I *am* the Immaculate Conception."

The name *is* the person.

What then, Jesus was asking the apostles, was the name which men had given him?

Some say John the Baptist, they told him, others Elias, others again, Jeremy or one of the prophets (Matt. 16:14).

[2] Phil. 2:10-11. The translation follows that of Father Kleist (*The New Testament,* rendered from the original Greek by James A. Kleist, S.J.; Milwaukee: Bruce, 1954).

These were all fine titles—John the Baptist, than whom none greater was born of woman; Elias, called by the Old Testament the Torch of God; Jeremias, the dour but majestic prophet with his terrible judgment upon the people immediately prior to the Babylonian captivity. All picked men. Dedicated men. God had spoken in them.

Jesus listened patiently, reflectively, to the answers of the twelve, nodding his head as they reported what they had heard. And then he asked bluntly, *Who do you say that I am?* (Matt. 16:15).

In this Jesus came directly to the point. The apostles must have been taken aback. There was a pause, an embarrassed one, probably, and then, finally, Simon gave a magnificent answer: *Thou art the Christ, the Son of the living God* (Matt. 16:16).

Simon was right. Simon had told Jesus his name, his true name, the one that Nicodemus came at night to ask about, the one which Pilate came close to learning but never did learn. On that day Simon made Jesus very happy. Anyone reading the gospels carefully can tell that that day was one of the high points of Jesus' life. It marked a turning point in Jesus' relations with his apostles. Things were much more intimate after that, and much more frank.[3]

[3] "From that time onwards Jesus began to make it known to his disciples that he must go up to Jerusalem, and there, with much ill usage from the chief priests and elders and scribes, must be put to death, and rise again on the third day" (Matt. 16:21).

Then Jesus fixed his gaze on Simon and said to him: *Blessed art thou, Simon son of Jona; it is not flesh and blood, it is my Father in heaven that has revealed this to thee* (Matt. 16:17). Then Jesus immediately added, as a direct consequence of what Peter had said, *And I tell thee this in my turn*—that is, you have told me my name, now I will tell you yours—*that thou art Peter* [the rock], *and it is upon this rock that I will build my church; and the gates of hell shall not prevail against it* (Matt. 16:18).

Even reading of this scene we feel, as Peter must have felt in the actuality of it, swept up by a great tide and hurled onto shores where vast conflicts are fought out in alternatives not less final than those of heaven and of hell. And all this teeters upon the thin figure of one man, whom, however, Jesus has named *The Rock*.

In its own degree this happening on the road to Philippi has been re-enacted in the lives of every one of us. To us as well the name of Jesus was revealed, not by flesh and blood but by the Father in heaven. We professed that name, that person, in the totality of his life and work, in our Baptism and in our Confirmation. If these sacraments were given to us when we were too young to know properly what it was all about, well, we cannot give that excuse any longer. We must speak for ourselves now and give answer: Who do *we* say Christ is?

Of course, when we say that Christ is the Lord, we do not know exactly what this will entail for us.

Peter didn't know what the future would bring when he said, *Thou art the Christ, the Son of the living God.*

Saul didn't know how Jesus would answer when Paul would become his name and he volunteered, *Lord, what wilt thou have me do?* (Acts 9:6).

Nor, at a still earlier moment of God's dealing with his people, did Samuel know for what he was offering himself when he went into the temple, in answer to the voice calling his name, and said, *Speak on, Lord, thy servant is listening* (I Kings 3:10).

But that is precisely the point. Are we giving ourselves to Christ, or making an investment? It is part of our acceptance of Christ—and the best part, too—that we accept him on these terms of not knowing all that the future holds.

During the Middle Ages the ceremony of fealty required the knight or serf to come forward to the dais on which sat the lord of the manor and place his hands joined within the hands of his lord. The question was put, "Do you promise obedience?" . . . *These hands which are man's prolongation of himself into his world and the tools of his shaping the world, do you give them to me?*

Every loyal knight answered unreservedly, "I promise."

This is the same ceremony used in the rites of Holy Orders today. The candidate comes before the bishop. He lays his hands, anointed now, in those of Christ's vicar, the successor of the apostles. The bishop closes his hands upon them. The question is put, "Do you promise obedience?" The newly ordained priest answers, "I promise."

What more can one offer? What greater allegiance can one profess than this unbounded confidence in Jesus our Lord? And then, how it breeds peace in our hearts! We know to whom we belong. We have a goal directing us, not an abstract goal but a person, who forgives if we falter on our way. Christ chose us through Baptism. In Confirmation we receive the strength to choose him. The two go together: *My sheep are known to me, and know me* (John 10:14).

8. *Witness*

... The Holy Spirit will come upon you, and you will receive strength from him; you are to be my witnesses in Jerusalem and throughout Judaea, in Samaria, yes, and to the ends of the earth. (Acts 1:8)

Theologians have chosen different ways to express the special character of what might be called the externalizing grace of Confirmation. Some have stressed the conferring or increase of the seven gifts of the Holy Spirit. Others follow the lead of St. John in his first letter, accenting the role of the Spirit in leading us to fullness of understanding, for he is the *spirit of truth* (I John 4:6).

But the different opinions keep this common element, that Confirmation puts the Christian face to face with his world. It is a social sacrament. It catches the Christian at the moment of his beginning to influence his world. It says to him, "Wait a minute! Take me along, you'll need me." Confirmation deals with *martyrium*, with "witnessing." It confers a special participation in the apostolic mission of Christ.

In a sermon to his converts St. Cyril of Jerusalem said,

The Holy Spirit is near to sign your soul with his seal. He will give you his heavenly badge, which makes the devils tremble. He will animate you for the fight. He will give you strength. . . . He will be your scout and protector, he will watch over you as over his own soldier.

But at this point we must be very careful. There is a temptation inherent in meditating upon one's apostolic mission in the kingdom of Christ. It is the temptation to slip mentally from the true and valid determination to do great things for Christ to the false and unrealistic supposition that great means will be required to do them. This is where Satan would like us to go astray, for he is very fond of a type of spiritual day-dreaming which is as dangerous—or as innocuous—as any other. It consists in imagining a Christian life fraught with mortal challenge. It leads us to think, when in connection with the sacrament of Confirmation we hear such terms as "shield," "soldier," "struggle," that our citizenry in Christ's kingdom will be constantly under mobilization. This is true often enough to lend the thought substance. On the whole, however, our witness as Christians will not be a dashing, military affair. It will be not so much a crucifixion or a crusade as the taking up of a daily cross.

It will be, come to think of it, a continuation of the *characteristic* quality of Christ's own apostolate. It will be the portrayal in our lives of that quality which will lead men to look at us and see that Christ is still visibly at work in the world.

But what is characteristic of Christ's apostolate? What set him off publicly as the awaited of the nations? When we discover the distinctive manner of Christ's own apostolate, we will know upon what model ours must be formed. We will know, therefore, what is the field where the grace of Confirmation finds its most significant application.

One day, during the early stages of his ministry, Jesus decided to return to Nazareth, his home town. Perhaps he felt that these fellow citizens of his deserved to hear before others the good news of who he was. It would be a surprise for them. They had known him as a boy, as a workman in his father's shop. They did not really know his name, as Peter would know it later. Still, these people had heard, perhaps more than others, the rumors of Jesus' impressive teaching. They would not be wholly unprepared. Jesus would make sure to choose for them a criterion which would leave no room for doubt. They would not be able to say, after his departure, that they were not sure. They would know for certain what at least he claimed to be.

And Jesus came back to Galilee with the power of the Spirit upon him; word of him went round through all the neighbouring country, and he began to preach in their synagogues, so that his praise was on all men's lips.

Then he came to Nazareth, where he had been brought up; and he went into the synagogue there, as his custom was, on the sabbath day, and stood up to read. The book given to him was the book of the prophet Isaias; so he opened it, and found the place where the words ran:

The Spirit of the Lord is upon me; he has anointed me, and sent me out to preach the gospel to the poor, to restore the brokenhearted; to bid the prisoners go free, and the blind have sight; to set the oppressed at liberty, to proclaim a year when men may find acceptance with the Lord, a day of retribution.

Then he shut the book, and gave it back to the attendant, and sat down. All those who were in the synagogue fixed their eyes on him, and thus he began speaking to them, This scripture which I have read in your hearing is to-day fulfilled. (Luke 4:14-21)

When Jesus wanted to say what it was that marked him out as the Messiah, he chose the sign of his apostolate among the poor, among the oppressed, among the little people of the world.

We have heard that the Sermon on the Mount is the charter of the Christian message. It embarrasses us. We do not like to read such phrases: *Blessed are the poor. . . . Blessed are the meek. . . . Blessed are those who suffer persecution for justice's sake. . . .* But we have not read the Old Testament very carefully, nor the New either for that matter, if we think that the Sermon on the Mount burst upon the ears of the Jews as an entirely new and unheard of statement of God's regard for man and man's relations with God. Many of Jesus' listeners were quite familiar with the ideas he spoke of. God doesn't change overnight his way of acting. God's revelation up to this time had been a preparation for this moment, and was united to it as the beginning of a sentence is to the end, where the last word not only completes but illumines all that has gone before.

The fact is that the poor have always been God's favorites.

He liked to choose younger children, the ones which the civil laws of those days least regarded. Abel was a younger son; his sacrifice was pleasing, Cain's wasn't. Jacob was a younger son and took the birthright from his brother Esau. Most especially, David was a younger son, in fact the last of eight boys. When the prophet Samuel came to Jesse's house where God was to point out to him Saul's successor, David was not even called from the fields. Samuel realized that something was not right; he learned somehow that there was yet another son. David was sent for. When the boy entered the room, still wearing his shepherd's cloak and carrying the home-made lyre with which he whiled away his shepherd's hours, the Lord said to Samuel, *Up, anoint him; this is my choice* (I Kings 16:12).

It had always been the pattern of God to choose those

who were despised in the eyes of the world. The women who had no children and who therefore were looked down upon by their contemporaries were the ones chosen for God's special work. Anna, Samuel's mother, had been sterile. Sara, Abraham's wife, had never had children. Rachel, Jacob's wife, could have no children, until God removed the shameful stigma and gave her Joseph as her firstborn. Elizabeth, the mother of John the Baptist, was already in her old age before a son was granted her.

God had his favorites. They were the poor, the despised, the neglected, the unregarded, the unimportant, the dispossessed of this world's goods.

Following this it is no surprise to learn that an obscure village maid will be the mother of the Most High.

> My soul magnifies the Lord,
> My spirit has found joy in God, who is my
>   Savior,
> because he has looked graciously upon the low-
>   liness of his handmaid. . . .
> he has put down the mighty from their seat, and
>   exalted the lowly;
> he has filled the hungry with good things, and
>   sent the rich away empty-handed. (Luke
>   1:46-48, 52-53)

This preoccupation of God with the little people of the world was not, in other words, a passing phase or pe-

ripheral aspect of his dealings with men. It was at the
heart of his revelation, it was the constant pattern of
his coming into history.

Jesus showed that repeatedly in his own life.

The criterion of his Messiahship which he gave the
Nazarenes was that of his apostolate among the poor.
To the disciples of John the Baptist when they came to
ask if he was indeed the expected one Jesus repeated the
lesson.

> Go and tell John what your own eyes and ears have
> witnessed; how the blind see, and the lame walk, and
> the lepers are made clean, and the deaf hear; how the
> dead are raised to life, and the poor have the gospel
> preached to them. (Luke 7:22)

It wasn't necessary to listen to Jesus' words to know
this. His actions showed it plainly enough.

He not only allowed himself to be invited to the table
of sinners, he even cultivated their friendship, as in the
case of Zachaeus. And he was severely criticized for it.
This really was a shocking thing. After all, such people
were the public enemies of God and the Hebrew faith.

We tell ourselves that such persons—Zachaeus, Simon,
and their crowd—must have been pretty good fellows
after all—diamonds in the rough, really—and that
Jesus knew this and that it was only the selfish or jealous
obstinacy of certain people who could not appreciate

the fact. We make the case too easy. These people were the outcasts of society and the despised of their town simply because they deserved to be. They were insolent, rude, selfish, cowardly, miserly; the oppressors of widows and orphans (especially the publicans among them), compromisers with the Roman occupation authorities, traitors possibly; proud, supercilious, supremely self-satisfied. The priests and the people weren't simply being squeamish when they complained of our Lord's hobnobbing with publicans and sinners. And Jesus did not answer by saying that they were not sinners really but nice chaps when you got to know them. They too, he said, were sons of Abraham, and the Son of Man had come precisely for this, *to search out and save what was lost* (Luke 19:9-10).

There are some remarkable lessons to be uncovered in a careful reading of our Lord's description of the last judgment, as we find it in the twenty-fifth chapter of St. Matthew, verses 31 to 41. There is first of all the whole interchange between our Lord and the men gathered from all corners of the globe, and a repetitious accenting of such things as feeding the hungry and clothing the naked and visiting those who are sick or in prison.

The men who stand before the judge seem quite surprised to learn that these things are important, in fact, supremely important, in fact—and now we are surprised —the difference between heaven and hell.

Then our Lord says, *Believe me, when you did it to one*

of the least of my brethren here, you did it to me (Matt. 25:40).

How have we been accustomed to read this sentence, and in particular that word *when*? Have we not adopted more or less automatically an interpretation which would go something like this: "I do kind things to Christ in doing kind things for others; I do especially kind things when I do them for the poor and the helpless"? This is a pleasant interpretation, but it is not what the sentence says. The word so vaguely translated "when" means in reality "to the degree that," "in so far as," and the correct interpretation of the sentence shows that it is not an exhortation urging an heroic charity towards the poor and outcasts of this world, but rather a blunt warning that if we do not offer the charity of our service to the poor, then we do not offer it to Christ: *To the degree that you did it to one of the least of my brethren here, you did it to me.* Both Origen and St. Thomas saw the difficulty and hastened to say that the clause does not exclude a charity offered even to the powerful of this world; this too can be genuine charity, done to Christ. Yes, it can. But it is not sufficient, and one does not begin there, for the whole tenor of the passage is clear: if we do not offer Christian charity to the poor and helpless, then we have not offered it to Christ. And on that last point rests our entire case.

Well now, we hasten to add to ourselves, of course these words of our Lord have to be *understood*—which is true enough, so long as our understanding does not become an explaining away. Then, too, there certainly are other ways of going to hell, like fornication, for example, or murder. Which is true enough, provided we continue to rank them only as *other* ways.

All of this is true and needs to be said. But the fact remains that when *Christ our Lord* wanted to talk about the acts which brought man either into full loving union with himself or earned him an eternity separated from God *he* chose to speak in terms of feeding or not feeding the hungry, clothing or not clothing the naked, visiting or not visiting the sick and the imprisoned.

Even so, we should have known.

Isaias, whose lips had been cleansed with a burning coal so that they might speak worthily the divine accents, often berated the self-styled righteous people of his own day, because they sought refuge in fasts and generous contributions. God said:

Nay, fast of mine is something other. The false claim learn to forego, ease the insupportable burden, set free the over-driven; away with every yoke that galls! Share thy bread with the hungry, give the poor and the vagrant a welcome to thy house; meet thou the naked, clothe him; from thy own flesh and blood turn not away.

Then sudden as the dawn, the welcome light shall break on thee . . . divine favour shall lead thee on thy journey. . . . The Lord will listen to thee when thou callest on him;

cry out, and he will answer, I am here at thy side. (Is.
58:6-9)

Jesus' . . . *you did it to me* is a perfect echo and fulfillment of this. *Cry out, and he will answer, I am here at
thy side*—here among these little ones, these despised and
neglected ones, these unfortunate people of the world.

We must not misread Isaias' criticism of fasting and
almsgiving. He says, not that these are not good and
necessary, but that they are not sufficient, especially if
circumstances suggest other actions much more important. Usually, contributions in money do form our normal exercise of charity, when that word is taken to mean
help for the poor. There is a long tradition in the Church,
in the letters of St. Paul, in the apostolate of Christ
himself, as well as in the Old Testament, urging us to
fulfill this duty. We try to do so, we try to do so with
good grace. A priest cannot forbear adding that both
attempts are usually admirably successful.

Have we nothing, then, to reproach ourselves with?

True, our attitude in giving money may offer some
food for thought, and we might seek occasions for that
personal attentiveness which means more than cash. It is
heartening to see young people, who do not have much
money in any case at their disposal, visiting orphanages,
taking the children on outings; or entertaining the
children and sick persons in the wards of our chronically
understaffed hospitals; or sitting by the bedside of the

aged, listening with great humility and respect to their empty, rambling narratives. Perhaps later, when they are married and have children and aged parents of their own, they may recall those college days of high generosity. They may then take into their home for vacation time, or even for good, one of those orphans who, for perhaps obvious reasons, never got adopted. They may give a welcome to someone removed by the courts from the company of his natural parents. They may, through agencies devoted to this purpose, support a refugee child, give a ray of hope to an otherwise empty existence.

There is a good chance that such young people will ask themselves, for this is a most timely question, how much a weight does racial prejudice, that almost typical Anglo-Saxon failing, toss into the balance of their judgments, actions, choice of words; and whether they, if the recording angel were to inquire, would be counted on the side of those who try to keep other people in a condition of second-class citizenship. How sad it is to hear of some who have been called to preach God's word claim that this same word has nothing against or even gives sanction to racial segregation. Even if it were true—and it is not true—it could only mean, following the whole tenor of God's work in the world, that the Christian should go the more promptly to the aid of those less well off than himself.

No, we must confess that time has not made Isaias' lesson less practical. He invites us to answer for ourselves: Do we claim something falsely against another? Are we trying to remove or at least to ease some burden galling to another? Have we ever given a homeless person welcome to our house? Do we visit the sick? Do we turn away from our own flesh and blood?

There is a paragraph from a sermon by Fr. Yves de Montcheuil, S.J., which expresses beautifully the point we are trying to make. It is worth remarking that Fr. de Montcheuil's life, or death rather, is as graphic an illustration as one could wish of what it means to bear this witness of Christ. During the Nazi occupation of France he was a member of the Resistance. He was captured eventually along with many of his group. A kindly German officer gave him the chance to admit to a charge which would only slightly compromise him in the eyes of the authorities: "And you were with these men, Father, momentarily and in passing as it were, for the sake of their spiritual welfare . . .?" Fr. de Montcheuil answered that they were his people, he was one of them. So, he was taken out that day along with "his people," and shot. Fr. de Montcheuil earlier had given a sermon on the feast of St. Thomas where he contrasted the attitudes taken towards truth by the Church and by certain political powers. The following citation is lifted from that sermon. Both the illustrations and the point of the paragraph have profound interest for us in thinking about the poor and the unfortunate:

The Greeks flattered themselves to have achieved the glorification of man; and yet in spite of this—or is it because of this?—we have the records of Greek cities which condemned to death children born deformed. In our own time the partisans of progress, in their misguided zeal, have renewed these classic aberrations and demanded that humanity, in its march to its goal, abandon to their lot the weak and infirm. They sneer at the charity which, in allowing them to live, shackles humanity with a dead weight.

But the Church acts in an entirely different fashion. She actively encourages young people of enthusiasm and high ideals to consecrate themselves entirely to the care of the aged and the sick, both in body and in soul, to the people from whom humanity can expect nothing more. Those young people might have opened up new avenues to an advancing mankind. But the Church loves man so much that every little bit of him, even if only the barest sign of him, is sacred to her. Nothing ever done for these little people of the world will ever appear too much to her. She knows well, the day that man has only disdain for those whom some have cruelly called cast-offs, that day all true love of humanity will have disappeared. There will remain, disguising itself under the name of humanitarianism and gathering to itself all the resources, only the egotism of the strong.

So it is then that those who love sincerely the truth, child of the Holy Spirit, are not those who agree to pay her homage only there where she shines in all her brilliance, but those for whom she is so dear that they would gather up everywhere the least fragments of her—everywhere, even when the stupidity and wickedness of man have rendered her hardly recognizable.

Those who don't have the courage to love her when she is deformed are not capable of having a pure love for her there where she shines forth in all her glory.[1]

Do we know why our witnessing of Christ and submission to the impulse of the Holy Spirit will be in direct proportion to our leaning down to assist the helpless of this world?

The answer is not this: . . . because in this way our charity was put to the test. It is not to afford us an occasion of heroism that the poor are always with us. To think so is to relegate the care of the dispossessed of this world's goods to the status of a work of supererogation, whereas the twenty-fifth chapter of St. Matthew clearly shows it to be the most fundamental work of all. Such an apostolate must be our normal condition as Christians.

Why then?

Because in this way we translate Christ's apostolate into the world. *We* were the helpless, in God's eyes. *We* were the cast-offs. But God leaned down to us. *The* statement of God's relationship to us—and hence of Christ's apostolate—is the expression of mercy—not merely

[1] Yves de Montcheuil, S.J., *Problèmes de Vie Spirituelle* (Paris: Editions de l'Epi, 1947), p. 143.

mercy, but long-suffering mercy, mercy not only above and beyond our merits but even against our merits.

To clothe the naked, to visit those who are sick and in prison, is our ideal because it is the truest statement of what we are. It is the most faithful translation of what God has done for us, and hence it is the most accurate witness of God at work in the world.

Eucharist

9. *Mass of the People*

The baptism of Jesus in the Jordan and the descending of the Holy Ghost upon him pointed toward Calvary. So, too, for the member of Christ's kingdom the sacraments of Baptism and Confirmation point toward the Mass. And just as Christ's death and resurrection lay at the center of his mission among men, so does the Mass lie at the center of our Christian living. Spiritually, we gravitate around the Mass. It gives us both force and order. We must try to understand it a little.

But the Mass is a mystery, which means that it belongs to the range of realities which man on his own can never either attain or adequately understand. This does not mean that we are absolved from thinking about the Mass. A lively faith always seeks understanding, and a mystery exists not in order to discourage us but to lead us on to the appreciation of further reaches in God's goodness towards men. That something is a mystery means not that we give up trying to understand but that we approach with reverence and a certain sense of wonder, and are content to understand something, though not all.

The Mass is a many-sided mystery. It contains the mystery of Christ's repeating in an unbloody manner the sacrificial act of Calvary, the mystery of the priest's representing both Christ and the people for whom the act is offered, the mystery of the people's sharing in this offering of Christ through his priest. Each of these aspects of the Mass asks for our attention. We must choose one of them. If we choose the last, it is not because this is the most profound aspect of the Mass, but because this aspect explores the part which the member of the Church, the baptized as such, plays at the offering of the Eucharistic sacrifice; and it is for the baptized as such that these meditations are written.

The Mass is, first of all, a liturgy. It is a stylized and symbolic action. It perdures over a certain length of time. It requires for its presentation a certain dimension in space. It is something played out like a drama, in words, gestures, and movement. All this is an orchestration of the central act of the Mass, but it is far from being superfluous. It is even more than merely pedagogical. It is so that the people may see and, seeing, participate.

Especially over the last half century historians of theology have studied the origins and development of the liturgical action. They have pointed out that the Roman

Mass is an outgrowth of a reform and rubrical stabilization effected in the sixth century by Pope St. Gregory. There were five parts or sections to the Gregorian Mass. These are still present, and still rather clearly defined, in the Mass as we see it before us each Sunday in our parish church. The five parts are these: entrance rite, instruction, offering, Eucharistic prayer or "Thanksgiving," and communion.

In our present meditation we will use these five parts in turn as keys for the understanding of what it is that the people do at Mass. It would be easy to become bogged down in an array of historical details. We will try to avoid this pitfall. We will give some of the salient points, characteristic of the liturgical section, and then reflect, theologically, upon them. For the sake of clarity, and as a memory aid toward the recall of what each part of the Mass means for the people, we might rename those five parts of the Mass in this way: *The Mass is:*

> *an altar,*
> *a book,*
> *an offering,*
> *a person,*
> *a people.*

THE MASS IS AN ALTAR

The first part of the liturgical action begins with the preparations by the priest in the sacristy and is concluded with the oration or collect prayer.

In earlier times its characteristic feature was the processional of the bishop and his ministers from their residence to the place where the sacrifice was to be offered. Litanies were sung—petitions for the people, who answered at certain intervals, *Kyrie eleison, Christe eleison, Kyrie eleison*—"Lord, have mercy on us; Christ, have mercy on us; Lord, have mercy on us." Upon arrival at the place of worship the people sang a hymn whose verses set the tone of the Mass for that day. This has become the *introit*. The altar was prepared, blessed, reverenced.

Throughout this first part of the Mass there is a constant preoccupation with the place of worship and especially with the altar. There is the procession, the arranging of things upon and around the altar, bowing before the altar, kissing it, incensing it, with almost exaggerated attention.

Why?

In all ages and among all peoples an altar has represented a spot located in time and place where God was thought to be particularly present to his people. The word temple means a "holy place," a spot where God enters into history, listens to the petitions of his people, judges their sincerity, grants or refuses their requests. The altar or shrine marks holy ground.

We have an illustration of this in the twenty-eighth chapter of the Book of Genesis. Jacob finds it expedient to leave his home country and seek his fortune in the land of his kinsman, Laban. He travels all day on foot, each night he lays himself down by the side of the road, puts a stone under his neck, and sleeps.

One night Jacob has a dream. He dreams he sees a ladder extending up to heaven from the spot where he sleeps. He sees God and his angels going up and down upon the ladder, between heaven and this point of earth. The dream is a message for him. When he awakes in the morning he says, *Why, this is the Lord's dwelling-place, and I slept here unaware of it!* Jacob is afraid: ... *What a fearsome place is this!* ... *This can be nothing other than the house of God; This is the gate of Heaven!* (Gen. 28:16-17). In witness of this fact the patriarch sets up on that spot a stone and pours oil upon it. He calls this place *Bethel,* which means "House of God." Other travelers passing by now will see this stone and have reverence. The stone is an altar. People will know that this is a spot where God enters into history.

Now, what some mysterious presentiment has revealed to all people and what God began to tell Israel through the patriarch Jacob is fulfilled for us in Christ.

The meaning is not merely that the altar is the table on which the body and blood of Christ will rest. The altar itself stands for Christ. In reverencing the altar, in bending down to kiss it and to incense it, the priest in figure reverences Christ. The altar was consecrated in these terms. It has cut into it (or at least into the altar

stone) five little crosses representing the five wounds of
Christ, for the altar itself represents his body.

The altar *is* already Christ. The House of God for us
is not really a building. It is a person, it stands for a
person. It represents in symbolic fashion the person of
Christ, the Incarnate Word, dwelling among us. The
altar around which gather the people is the first sign
of his presence, and it reminds the people that the worship of God is not a vague, abstract, or spiritualized
thing, nor can aesthetic wanderings along valley trails
in beautiful fall weather substitute for it. The worship
of God is in a place, at a time. In order to partake of that
worship the people must be there, with reverence, for
God is there. The Mass is an altar.

THE MASS IS A BOOK

In the earliest days of the Church a clear distinction
was made between the celebration of the Eucharist and
another liturgical action which was called the *synaxis,*
a Greek word meaning "a coming together." The Eucharist was performed only on Sunday. The *synaxis*
normally preceded it but was clearly seen to be distinct,
because the *synaxis* was held also on Wednesday and
Friday, without being followed by the Eucharistic celebration. Soon the Eucharist was added to the week-day
synaxis. During the fourth century the fusion of the
two into one liturgical action became complete. The
Roman rite of Good Friday still shows in almost its

pure form a *synaxis* service followed by communion from the reserved Sacrament.

The *synaxis* is no more nor less than the Jewish synagogue service brought into the Christian liturgy. The parts are the same: reading from the Scriptures, psalmody, sermon or instruction, prayers. So it is that this portion of today's Mass revolves around the book instead of around the chalice, paten, or offerings. It reminds us of Christ's own apostolic method. In a passage to which we have already referred we have seen how Jesus, when he went back to Nazareth, entered the synagogue, took up the roll of the prophet Isaias, read from it, and commented upon it (Luke 4:14-30). It was his custom so to announce himself in a new town.

It was also the strategy of the apostles when they in their turn set out to spread the kingdom of God. Paul and Barnabas, on arriving at their destination, went first to the synagogue, if it were the sabbath day. This was a point of contact between themselves and the citizens of the city, not only Jewish but also pagan, for many of these latter were attracted to the Hebrew faith.

Paul and his companions. . . . passed on from Perge, and reached Pisidian Antioch, where they went and took their seats in the synagogue on the sabbath day. When the reading from the law and the prophets was finished, the rulers of the synagogue sent a message to them to say, Brethren, if you have in your hearts any word of encouragement for the people, let us hear it.

> Then Paul stood up, and made a gesture with his hand to claim audience. Listen, he said, men of Israel. . . . (Acts 13:13-16)

The first Christians, while adopting the specifically Christian Eucharist, kept the synagogue service as the instructional part, so to speak, of their worship— and the *synaxis* was really a worship; it was not a private "devotional" gathering. It was a public and highly official exercise of the liturgy. Only the faithful and the catechumens might attend, but these last were not allowed to stay for the last portion of the service, the prayers. The bishop presided. The deacons read from the Scriptures. It was the bishop, seated on his throne, who gave the sermon or instruction. No one without a special delegation could take his place in this. Even up to Augustine's time the rule was in force, not because of any greater talents on the part of the bishop, but because he pre-eminently stood in the place of Christ. He was the successor of the apostles and hence the chief guardian of the faith which they had implanted. He was not expected to give his personal opinions; it was the faith—"the unchanging 'saving' truth of the gospel, and not any personal opinion of his own, which he must proclaim in the liturgical sermon, because he alone was endowed by the power of the Spirit with the 'office' of speaking the authentic mind of his Church."[1]

[1] Dom Gregory Dix, *The Shape of the Liturgy* (London: Dacre Press: A & C Black Ltd., 1952), p. 40.

All this invites us to reflect that the Mass is meant to teach us our faith. The Spirit of Truth, who will bring us unto all truth, is active in the Church not merely in the pronouncements of Rome or in other lesser publications, but in the readings and instruction given at Mass. The Mass is in fact the sacramental model for all instruction. It reminds the priest that he was ordained to give instruction just as he was ordained to hear confessions and to offer the sacrifice. It reminds the people that growth in the knowledge of their faith is a part of their worship. Finally, for neither priest nor layman is it personal opinion that counts. The faith is the thing, even when its lessons are difficult. It is not beside the point to recall that many of the listeners of Jesus and of Paul did not like what they heard. Of course, those listeners were in a different position from us now. Even so, the book and the pulpit are not designed to tell us what we are curious to hear, nor even what we are capable of understanding, much less what our prejudices can take without shock; the book and the pulpit tell us rather what we need to know in order to be saved. The Mass is not a discussion club. It is the "good news" for those who have ears to hear.

THE MASS IS AN OFFERING

In many ways the offertory is the most "popular" part of the Mass, if popular be taken in its root meaning as that which pertains to and is carried on by the people.

The history of the offertory shows a remarkable fluidity and adaptability. There has always been room there for more personal sentiments than the central portion of the Eucharistic prayer itself had allowed. The Eucharistic prayer received its shape and order from our Lord himself, from the series of his actions—taking, blessing, breaking, and giving—at the Last Supper. The offertory, on the contrary, has received its determination from the practice of the people—from the bottom up, so to speak.

Whether what is now called the offertory procession was a primitive part of the liturgy of the Eucharist is no longer disputed. It seems clear that it wasn't. The Eastern rites did not have it, at least not at this place. It did not exist, apparently, in Rome in the third century when Hippolytus put on paper the terms of the special "office" or "liturgy" of the bishop.[2] It is equally clear, however, that the people began very early to show a desire to take a more active part in the Eucharistic action, and this not *before* the liturgy, as in the East, but *within* the liturgy, during the time of the preparation of the matter for sacrifice. This took the form of their bringing forward gifts, not only bread and wine but other gifts of harvest or workmanship. The deacons received the gifts from their hands and selected from them the elements of sacrifice which the bishop would consecrate. In these early days there was a clear division

[2] This is the conclusion of Dom Bernard Capelle, *A New Light on the Mass* (Dublin: Clonmore & Reynolds Ltd., 1952), p. 22.

of function. To offer the matter of sacrifice was the liturgical office of the laity. To receive it and prepare it was the office of the deacons. "To offer" (in the truest sense) and to consecrate was the office of the bishop and his presbyters.

The meaning is clear. The priest in our Mass now performs at the offertory those functions which the people formerly performed in their procession to the spot where the deacons received their gifts. The people, consequently, give to the priest a mandate to act in their name. Of course, they do not constitute him a priest, they do not give him the power to sacrifice; such a privilege has always in the history of God's dealings with his people been the initiative of God, not of man. But the people entrust to the priest, as to their intercessor and representative, the matter of sacrifice. In this way they both ratify and make concretely possible his acting before God on their behalf.

During those ages when an offertory procession enjoyed its vogue—as early as the fourth century in Rome, a bit later in Gaul and in Africa and up to the time of the Middle Ages—a great many prayers were composed for the use of the priest as he proceeded to carry out his functions. Some of these prayers were bound into volumes and thus given permanent form. From a collection of prayers at one time in the posession of Charles the Bald comes the offertory prayer the priest says as he lifts the paten: *Receive, Holy Father,*

*almighty and eternal God, this spotless host which I
thy unworthy servant offer to thee for my numberless
sins, offenses, and negligences.* . . . It was phrased as a
personal prayer, for an individual's use; this is the reason
for its still being in the first person singular, whereas
other prayers of the offertory, as indeed of the whole
Mass, are in the first person plural.

On the whole, the offertory is a clearly unified and
easily understood part of the Mass. Two points, however, must be made.

The first is this. The Mass is an oblation not in virtue
of the offertory but rather in virtue of the central
portion of the Mass, the Eucharistic prayer. The gestures
and prayers of the canon are our principal reason and
justification for calling the Mass an offering. These were
and are still the first offertory prayers. One in particular deserves mention here as holding a clear primacy
among them: the *Unde et memores* immediately following the consecration: *Wherefore, O Lord, we thy servants and likewise thy holy people, calling to mind* . . .
offer to thy sovereign majesty. . . . This is the most significant prayer of the Mass, because better and more
anciently than any other it expresses the essence of the
Eucharistic action—a *memorial* of Christ's death and
resurrection now offered once more by Christ as head
and the people as members.

However, just as in the canon, so also in the offertory
it is the whole Church which makes oblation. It is

always the whole Church which offers sacrifice, but each member according to his degree. The offertory has, for our present purpose, this pedagogical advantage over the canon: it makes plain the degree in which the people enter, through offering, upon the sacrifice itself.

This brings us to the second point which deserves stress in reflection upon the offertory. It is a more important point. It is to understand *what* the people offer.

There is a strange ambivalence in the words used in the offertory prayers. A careful reading discloses a marked tendency to treat the elements of sacrifice as though they were already transformed. The bread is called by the same term which is applied to it after the consecration—*this spotless host*. (Spotless here does not mean clean but "sinless.") Our prayer is that it may *profit us unto salvation*. The chalice is called the *chalice of salvation*. The whole oblation is then referred to as a *sacrifice prepared for thy holy Name*.

Dom Capelle sees in this tendency of the offertory prayers to anticipate the consecratory act an important theological lesson. He sees, not merely the unity of the offertory with the rest of the Mass, though that lesson is important enough, but also an aspect of the people's participation at Mass.

For, if the offertory shows a tendency to consider the elements as already transformed, then the people, in offering them, are not simply extrinsic to the sacrificial moment of the Mass, centered in the Eucharistic prayer.

They are already taken up into that transformation, but in an initial sense.

Dom Capelle puts it this way:

> The offertory . . . marks . . . the first moment of the sacrifice in the strict sense of the word. . . . It is the whole oblation, but only in its preparation. A perfect preparation, exteriorly and interiorly. . . . In one sense nothing has been done, and yet everything has been done. It is like the case of the candidate for monastic profession; an hour before, nothing has been done, the sacramental act has not yet been accomplished; and yet everything has been done: the novice has already made the offering in his heart, and the chart of the profession has been written. The offertory is not a *partial* act having *absolute* value; it is rather a *complete* act, but a *relative* one.[3]

Our lesson, then, is this: It is true that it is a part of the laity's prayerful assistance at Mass for the people to make in their hearts an offering of their own persons, of all their actions, hopes, ambitions. It is true that the offering of bread and wine—now itself symbolized by monetary offerings—is the sign of this interior oblation. These are worthy and perhaps indispensable aspects of the total concept of the Mass. They are not, however, the

---

[3] *Ibid.*, pp. 26-27. The offertory is not an act with a value, even a partial value, separable from the whole of the liturgical action. The offertory has value in God's eyes precisely *in as much as* it is an offering of that which is about to become God's Son.

best expression of what is happening liturgically and, as it were, independently of personal piety.

For, if Dom Capelle is right in thinking that the oblation act of the offertory is already rich with the oblation acts of the canon, then *what* the people offer is not primarily bread and wine, nor even primarily themselves; *what* the people offer is Christ, here at the offertory in an initial and anticipated moment of that fullness of presence which is his a little later in virtue of the consecratory prayers which only the priest can say.

In this merciful manner has God undertaken to relieve the spiritual poverty of his people:

> . . . however poor or however fervent our participation in the sacrifice of the Mass may be, our personal worth is not the measure of the value of our action. The Mass is not our act in the same sense as an alms or the recitation of a *Pater* is our act. The Mass is the act of the whole Church and above all the act of Christ who is its Head. I am permitted to collaborate in this act which existed before me, outside me and without me. I intervene in it in all timidity.[4]

These remarks need to be complemented by what we will say in the fourth section.

THE MASS IS A PERSON

The earliest name for the Mass, as a distinct liturgical action, was *eucharistia,* which might be translated as

[4] *Ibid.*, p. 19.

the "Eucharistic Prayer," or, more accurately, "Thanksgiving." The term referred to the total liturgical action, from the preparation of the elements for sacrifice, which is now the offertory, to the communion.

The central moment of this action from the very beginning was, of course, the consecration. The consecration implied the offertory and the communion. It still does, its own place in the Mass is incomplete without them. It is a keystone, it is the most important thing, it is the reality in the Mass which makes the sacrifice availing unto our salvation. That's why this part of the Mass might simply be called, *The Person.*

With the preface the priest moves into that portion of the liturgy which is particularly his. He grows silent, as though he were alone with God in the holy of holies. Nevertheless, the prayers he says are still in the first person plural. He is there not as an individual but as the representative of the people.

What is the part of the people at this moment of the Mass?

In the present condition of theological learning one would be rash to claim a definitive answer to that question. Following the lead of Dom Capelle, we might bring one ray of light upon the problem.

At the same time that the priest is the representative of the people he is also the representative of Christ. "The same priest, the same oblation, the same victim," says the Council of Trent of the identity of the Mass with

Christ's death on Calvary. But Christ is here, working through his priest, under a special title—that of head of the Mystical Body. Our baptism has brought us into union with Christ, head of the Church, and in union therefore with him who is both high priest and victim of the sacrificial act. We are members of him who has given to the priest the power to sacrifice. This is the exercise of that royal priesthood to which our baptism has introduced us.

> By the waters of baptism, as by common right, Christians are made members of the Mystical Body of Christ the Priest, and by the "character" which is imprinted on their souls, they are appointed to give worship to God; thus they participate, according to their condition, in the priesthood of Christ.[5]

Thus the people enter, through Christ, upon some aspect even of the sacrificial act at Mass, indirectly but in a real manner. But this is not all.

Because Christ is head, when Christ is offered to the Father, we are offered in him. Dom Gregory Dix has transcribed for us a passage from Augustine which defies improving:

> The city of the redeemed itself, the congregation and society of the saints, is offered as an universal sacrifice to

[5] Pius XII, "On the Sacred Liturgy," ed. Gerald Ellard, S.J. (New York: The America Press, 1948), p. 44.

God by the High-priest, Who offered even Himself in
suffering for us in the form of a servant, that we might
be the Body of so great a Head. . . . This is the sacrifice of
Christians, "the many one Body in Christ." Which thing
also the church celebrates in the sacrament of the altar,
familiar to the faithful, wherein it is shewn to her that in
this thing which she offers she herself also is offered to
God.[6]

What do we have of our own that would be of value
to God the Father? Nothing. But are we therefore ex-
cluded from the range of those things which God finds
pleasing? Is there nothing in our world which can make
God smile upon us as He once smiled upon and blessed
all creation in its dawning? We are offered to God the
Father in his Son. *Through him and with him and in
him is to thee, Father almighty, in the unity of the holy
Spirit, all honor and glory.*

There is a poem of Charles Péguy which expresses,
though in another connection, this favorite Pauline
theme of our being borne along by Christ into the presence of the Father. It is called "A Vision of Prayer" and is
published in Julian Green's selection from Péguy's
poems entitled *God Speaks*. God is talking, to himself,
as it were. He is commenting upon a strange, tremen-
dous fleet which he watches sailing towards him over
the seas. It is a vast fleet of prayer, in formation like
the point of a spear. The lead ship is a mighty *Our Fa-*

[6] *De. civ. Dei x*, 6; Dix, *op. cit.*, p. 248.

ther voiced by God's own Son, who joins his hands in front of him, making the bow which first breaks the ocean's turbulent waves. In his wake come the other ships, line upon line of them, of all different shapes and sizes, some riding high and proud, others very humble and low in the water. All of them glide steadily in the wake of Christ, even those so far away they may have lost sight of the fact that they too are in a formation. *This is the fleet,* God the Father says, *which I cannot resist.*

We had occasion earlier to point out that our personal measure of fervor or achievement is not the chief value at work in our assisting at Mass. We are members of Christ, that is our boast.

> God has in this manner come to the aid of the profound wretchedness of man. He responded to our secret need not to be dependent on the possibilities of our own poor personality; to be supported by some more solid foundation than that of our own little measure of good will; to surpass our natural capacity, supported and borne along by an infinite force.[7]

The fourth part of the Mass ends with the priest's taking up the Sacred Host, making several little crosses of blessing with it over the chalice, and then raising them both together in what is called the "little elevation." *Through him and with him and in him,* he says,

---

[7] Capelle, *op. cit.,* p. 19.

*is to thee, Father almighty, in the unity of the Holy
Spirit, all honor and glory.* To this statement and to all
that has preceded it the people answer a resounding
Amen! So be it!

THE MASS IS A PEOPLE

It is not sufficient to say of the Mass that Jesus Christ
is really present, body and blood, soul and divinity. It
must be added that he is present under the form of food.
He is meant to be taken as food. Every Mass, to be
complete, must have communion, at least that of the
priest.

The communion portion of the Mass really begins
with the Our Father, which all through the centuries
has been a prayer particularly associated with the dis-
tribution of communion.

There is a reason for this, and the reason is the same
one that has led us to call this part of the Mass *a people.*

If someone were to ask us what the word communion
means, we would probably answer, "union with," and
go on to explain, "union with Christ." This of course
is a true answer, but it was not the one which first
struck the consciousness of the faithful. The earliest
meaning of communion in the liturgy is union not first
of all of the members with Christ but of the members
with each other. True, this union is accomplished in
Christ and has its worth in Christ. But it means, in its
first historical usage, fraternal union among the baptized.

This is why the *Our Father*, the pre-eminent prayer of fraternal union, is so closely associated with the Eucharist. "*Our* Father. . . . forgive us . . . *as we forgive* those. . . ."

It is why the deacon, in earlier centuries, would at this point admonish the people in a loud voice that none who were engaged in quarrel with other members of the faith should approach the holy table. For such a one to receive the sacrament of unity is a manifest contradiction. *If thou art bringing thy gift, then, before the altar, and rememberest there that thy brother has some ground of complaint against thee, leave thy gift lying there before the altar, and go home; be reconciled with thy brother first, and then come back to offer thy gift* (Matt. 5:23-24).

The custom of the kiss of peace has been reserved now to solemn Masses and then to the ministers alone. But its spirit is the same as that of the *Our Father* and of the deacon's admonition. It is a ratification by gesture of what St. Paul said of the Lord's supper: *Is not the bread we break a participation* [i.e., a corporate sharing] *in Christ's body? The one bread makes us one body, though we are many in number; the same bread is shared by all* (I Cor. 10:16-17).

One does not therefore approach the communion table (and would that our architects would realize that the altar is a table!) as an individual, but as a member of a body. In the communion of her members the Church as a whole communicates. Her children are there, not as isolated units, but as branches grafted to the one true vine, sharing the same life that courses in each one's veins. It is their baptism which has brought them together. It is communion which vivifies their communal existence.

> Whoever wishes to have life knows henceforth in whom he must live, from whom he must have life. Let him approach and believe. He must allow himself to be incorporated in order to be vivified. . . . He must be careful not to become himself a putrefied member which must be amputated. He must not be a false member, and become an object of shame. Rather must he be a member which is at once fine, apt, and strong. He must be perfectly united to the body. Then he will live in God and for God.[8]

The significant thing about this quotation from St. Augustine is that he is attributing here to holy communion the effect which we usually, by omission, confine to baptism: the building up of the Church, the incorporation of the members into Christ. Thus, St. Augustine reminds us that in receiving at the altar table we become *more* a Church, *more* a people of God, because more closely united to him who is head.

The Eucharist is exercised within the Church; the

[8] This passage from St. Augustine is cited by Dom Capelle, p. 56.

Church on the other hand grows out of the Eucharist. There is here a marvelous reciprocity and another instance of that supernatural truth which St. Augustine expressed so perfectly: in him all that is scattered in us is brought into one.

CONCLUDING REMARK

In a late period of the history of the Mass, the opening verses of St. John's gospel were added after the blessing and dismissal. The custom spread rapidly, for the faithful must have perceived that the prologue of St. John's gospel was an expressive summary not merely of the Mass but of the whole mystery of the redemption, of which the Mass is a sacramental re-presentation.

St. John's prologue details the downward motion inherent in God's creating a world and then sending his Son down into it not as a stranger but as himself one of its citizens. And how the Son brought, for those who would believe in him, the power to become themselves the sons of God, and how in this way the Son began, first of all in himself, and then in us, the upward motion of man and creation back to the Father. And how we have seen his glory, the glory belonging to the only-begotten Son of the Father, full of grace and truth.

We, too, at Mass have seen that glory, which is Christ himself. We are his witnesses, not with our eyes only, for that is too passive a witness, but with our hands, our heads, our hearts. We have received him into ourselves, and so we too have begun the upward motion to the Father. We know where our true home is. We know how to get there.

10. *Eucharistic Man*

"... in him the Church learns to offer herself."
(St. Augustine, *de civ. Dei* x,20)

The Church is not being merely arbitrary in insisting, under pain of mortal sin, that Catholics be present at Mass at least every Sunday and holyday. She knows that there is an essential connection between being a Christian and assisting at the Lord's supper. The reason ultimately is twofold: that the Mass is at once the source as also the pattern of Christian living.

We have heard often enough that the Mass is a source of grace and strength to us. It is important now to consider the other aspect of this meaning in the Mass: that it not only gives us the strength but shows us as well *how* to live.

What has happened in the Eucharist, really?

Simple, ordinary elements have been offered and transformed. Bread and wine are the common denomi-

nator of food in the world. There is nothing special
about them; over the centuries the bread for sacrifice has
never turned into cake nor the wine into champagne,
even though the churches in which they were offered
grew more and more splendid.

But there is at least this to remark about the sacrificial elements: they do not grow like that in nature,
they are the products of man's labor. It is a simple,
uncomplicated labor. It is one which seems to be almost
instinctive in man. The bread and wine are redolent of
earth and man's struggle with it in the sweat of his brow.
It was the struggle which made him a man, in the virile
sense. So too it is his struggle which has made the earth
and its produce into something worth offering to God.
And these simple elements, these everyday products
of uncomplicated labor, are the things which become
the vehicles of God. They become supremely important.
God is present to us in them as he is in no other way.

After their offering and transformation God does not
nod and say "Thank you, that's nice, I appreciate your
offering and I'll see you again some time." He says,
"Now that I have touched these gifts and transformed
them, I give them back to you. It is not just your labor
which interests me. It is you who need to be changed.
My Son can do that for you, as often as you eat his flesh
and drink his blood. Only my Son can do it. Don't go
away empty. I give him back to you."

It is this last, this participation in the body of Christ,

which forcibly reminds us that the Mass is not a sort of sticker plastered on our life's luggage. It is intrinsic to our life. It is the privileged moment, the concentration, the center, the intense heart, the representative act of our lives as members of the Church. It is not enough to say that without the Mass we *have* not something; without the Mass we *are* not something, in our very being as Catholics we grow precarious, vague, and begin to dissolve.

But it should be abundantly clear by now that the Eucharist does not offer to us a pattern of life merely as individuals. Who are we anyhow, so to be changed by receiving again our gifts transformed now into God's Son? Have we somehow shot out of the confining and sometimes demented limits of the times and places in which we live? Does the Eucharist want to turn us into angels?[1] This is not a new question. Here, as in so much else, Augustine is ahead of us: *And so, my brethren, let no one say, I am not of this world. Whoever you are, if you are man, you are of this world. But he who made the world has come to you. He has saved you from the world.*

Dom Gregory Dix points out in the book already cited that in the early ages of the Church it was necessary

---

[1] In a familiar hymn we sing of receiving "the bread of angels." It is not, however, the ethereal character, so to speak, of the angels' "bread" which is referred to, but rather its strength. A more accurate translation would be "the bread of the strong." This was the manna which gave the Hebrews in the desert force enough to withstand the dangers around them.

for the Church to teach men how to die, for their environment allowed the alternatives only of surrender or
death. But it is now, some centuries since, the task of the
Church to teach men how to live. She accomplishes
both tasks in the same way, in the Eucharist.

"We cannot live without celebrating the Lord's day,"
said the martyrs of North Africa to their judge in the
early fourth century. Later, when the persecutions had
come to an end, St. Augustine told his parishioners:

> Your mystery is laid on the table of the Lord, your
> mystery you receive. To that which you are you answer
> "Amen," and in answering you assent. For you hear
> the words [of administration]: "the body of Christ,"
> and you answer "Amen." Be a member of the Body of
> Christ that the *Amen* may be true. (Sermon 272)

To that which you are you answer "Amen." Become
what you are! The entire relationship of the Christian
with Christ is in those four words. For both to us and to
our world something has happened, yet not enough, and
even *what* has happened cries out for its fulfillment.
*It is the Lord's death that you are heralding, whenever
you eat this bread and drink this cup, until he comes*
(I Cor. 11:26). At the Eucharistic table we look both
backwards and forwards and yet are completely ab-
sorbed in the tension of the present. Our present,
precisely, is rich with tradition and pledge. Theologians
will say, in brief of all this, that the Eucharist is escha-

tological, or, in simpler terms, that the Eucharist is the perpetual coming of the risen Christ into history, of triumph into struggle, of eternity into time. Our categories begin to dissolve in the near approach of God. *Everything is for you, whether it be Paul, or Apollo, or Cephas, or the world, or life, or death, or the present, or the future; it is all for you, and you for Christ, and Christ for God* (I Cor. 3:22-23).

All this bears explanation, this coming of Christ into our time and place. What can it mean?

Let us not delude ourselves. It means first of all sacrifice. The substance of bread, the substance of wine had to disappear. Christ is judge, not by anything which he says or does but by what he *is*. His coming is the constant crisis, the sifting and winnowing of the world. Our world is not indifferent to Christ, or merely passive in his presence. No more than that of Rome was. The world is hostile, not as something outside us, but inside us. The world is mixed up within us with what Christ has accomplished. "These two cities [of God and the world] are confounded together in this world and are utterly mingled with each other, until they be wrenched apart by the final judgment" (*de civ. Dei* i, 35). The first battlefield—and the last—is that of our own hearts.

On the other hand, a member of the Church cannot be dismal. Eucharist even as a word means "Thanksgiving," still more as an action is it suffused with joy. The Eucharist is the renewal of the angelic *Gloria*, the

Te Deum of the people for beginning each working day.

For one who believes that Christ is the Lord, every hour is a joyous last hour. This is true not merely because each day brings its free decisions which shape our personalities unto eternity; eternity is not really future. It is not eternity which is changed in the Eucharist, but the present. Eternity has got all mixed up in time, more so than the evil and hostility of the world have got mixed up in the good. It is time now that has a new dimension, has it *now,* does not need to wait till the end of the world to acquire it. That is why even now we can be joyous. We do not need to wait. We are joyous because each day brings its own incarnation of Christ into our Churches, into our hearts, into our lives.

The man for whom the Eucharist is not a pageant, however wondrous, but rather the representative act of his being as member of the Church will not flee the challenge of his times, when affairs have become, in Christopher Fry's virile phrase, "soul-size." But then again he will not succumb to them. He will not lose sight of what happened in the past to give him this moment, nor of that future happening, of which this moment is a pledge. He will be in the world as one possessing though not possessed, as one transforming but not himself transformed, unless it be into Christ.

Perhaps no one has put this better than Dom Gregory

Dix, and his statement sums up nicely the Eucharistic function which the Christian has in the world:

> Over against the dissatisfied "Acquisitive Man" and his no less avid successor the dehumanized "Mass-Man" of our economically focussed societies insecurely organized for time, Christianity sets the type of "Eucharistic Man"—man giving thanks with the product of his labours upon the gifts of God, and daily rejoicing with his fellows in the worshipping society which is grounded in eternity. This is man to whom it was promised on the night before Calvary that he should henceforth eat and drink at the table of God and be a king. That is not only a more joyful and more humane ideal. It is the divine and only authentic conception of the meaning of all human life, and its realization is in the Eucharist.[2]

The next to last words of the Bible are these:

> *Be it so, then; come, Lord Jesus* (Apoc. 22:20).

[2] Dix, *op. cit.*, xviii-xix.